ROMANS

The Gospel of Grace

A STUDY OF ROMANS 1-8

by

KRISTIN SCHMUCKER

Thank you for choosing this study to help you dig into God's Word. We are so passionate about women getting into Scripture, and we are praying that this study will be a tool to help you do that. Here are a few tips to help you get the most from this study:

- Before you begin, take time to look into the context of the book. Find out who wrote it and learn about the cultural climate it was written in, as well as where it fits on the biblical timeline. Then take time to read through the entire book of the Bible we are studying if you are able. This will help you to get the big picture of the book and will aid in comprehension, interpretation, and application.

- Start your study time with prayer. Ask God to help you understand what you are reading and allow it to transform you (Psalm 119:18).

- Look into the context of the book as well as the specific passage.

- Before reading what is written in the study, read the assigned passage! Repetitive reading is one of the best ways to study God's Word. Read it several times, if you are able, before going on to the study. Read in several translations if you find it helpful.

- As you read the text, mark down observations and questions. Write down things that stand out to you, things that you notice, or things that you don't understand. Look up important words in a dictionary or interlinear Bible.

- Look for things like verbs, commands, and references to God. Notice key terms and themes throughout the passage.

- After you have worked through the text, read what is written in the study. Take time to look up any cross-references mentioned as you study.

- Then work through the questions provided in the book. Read and answer them prayerfully.

- Paraphrase or summarize the passage, or even just one verse from the passage. Putting it into your own words helps you to slow down and think through every word.

- Focus your heart on the character of God that you have seen in this passage. What do you learn about God from the passage you have studied? Adore Him and praise Him for who He is.

- Think and pray through application and how this passage should change you. Get specific with yourself. Resist the urge to apply the passage to others. Do you have sin to confess? How should this passage impact your attitude toward people or circumstances? Does the passage command you to do something? Do you need to trust Him for something in your life? How does the truth of the gospel impact your everyday life?

- We recommend you have a Bible, pen, highlighters, and journal as you work through this study. We recommend that ballpoint pens instead of gel pens be used in the study book to prevent smearing.

Here are several other optional resources that you may find helpful as you study:

- www.blueletterbible.org This free website is a great resource for digging deeper. You can find translation comparison, an interlinear option to look at words in the original languages, Bible dictionaries, and even commentary.

- A Dictionary. If looking up words in the Hebrew and Greek feels intimidating, look up words in English. Often times we assume we know the meaning of a word, but looking it up and seeing its definition can help us understand a passage better.

- A double-spaced copy of the text. You can use a website like www.biblegateway.com to copy the text of a passage and print out a double-spaced copy to be able to mark on easily. Circle, underline, highlight, draw arrows, and mark in any way you would like to help you dig deeper and work through a passage.

Let's Memorize Romans chapter 8!

Romans 8 has been called the greatest chapter in all of the Bible. It is a chapter full of hope and a chapter full of practical encouragement for our Christian lives. There is nothing more powerful than the Word of God, and I can't think of a better passage to memorize than Romans 8. Through the course of the two-part study on Romans, you will be able to memorize the entire chapter of Romans 8. I think you will find that the time invested in memorizing this chapter will be a great comfort and encouragement to you. If you aren't in a season where memorizing the whole chapter is possible in the course of the study, choose a few verses or just go at a slower pace in memorizing the chapter.

Romans Vol. 1 Memory Schedule:

WEEK 1 *Romans 8:1-3*

WEEK 2 *Romans 8:4-6*

WEEK 3 *Romans 8:7-9*

WEEK 4 *Romans 8:10-11*

WEEK 5 *Romans 8:12-14*

WEEK 6 *Romans 8:15-16*

WEEK 7 *Romans 8: 17-18*

WEEK 8 *Romans 8: 19-21*

HELPFUL TIPS FOR
Scripture Memorization

- Read the verse repetitively.

- Meditate on the meaning of the verse.

- Instead of just memorizing the words, seek to allow them to penetrate your heart

- Pray the verse

- Think about what it teaches you about the character of God

- Think about how it applies to your life

- Think about what you know for sure after reading the verse

- Try writing out the verse to test your memory

- Review the verses you have memorized often to keep them fresh

- Keep your verse with you throughout your day to review

- Recite the verse out loud

- Review multiple translations to better understand the verse

- Memorize the reference as well, so that you know where it is located

- Look up definitions of words that are unfamiliar

- Set the verse to music

- Memorize with a friend and keep each other accountable

- Read the context of the verse to get a better understanding of its meaning

- Study the verse in-depth

- Listen to the verse or entire passage on an audio Bible

- Have fun!

- Challenge yourself!

- Review. Review. Review.

THEMES IN *Romans*

As you study, use this section to summarize and record specific themes for each chapter.

Chapter 1 _____
_____
_____

Chapter 2 _____
_____
_____

Chapter 3 _____
_____
_____

Chapter 4 _____
_____
_____

Chapter 5 _____
_____
_____

Chapter 6 _____
_____
_____

Chapter 7 _____
_____
_____

Chapter 8 _____
_____
_____

Table of Contents

WEEK 1 2
    Rom. 8:1-3 Memory Verse 22
    Weekly Reflection 23

WEEK 2 26
    Rom. 8:4-6 Memory Verse 46
    Weekly Reflection 47

WEEK 3 50
    Rom. 8:7-9 Memory Verse 70
    Weekly Reflection 71

WEEK 4 74
    Rom. 8:10-11 Memory Verse 94
    Weekly Reflection 95

WEEK 5 98
    Rom. 8:12-14 Memory Verse 118
    Weekly Reflection 119

WEEK 6 122
    Rom. 8:15-16 Memory Verse 142
    Weekly Reflection 143

WEEK 7 146
    Rom. 8:17-18 Memory Verse 166
    Weekly Reflection 167

WEEK 8 170
    Rom. 8:19-21 Memory Verse 190
    Weekly Reflection 191

ADDITIONAL RESOURCES
    Outline & Flow of Themes in Romans 193
    Map of the Roman Empire 194
    Word Study: Justification & Sin 195
    Echoes of Israel in the Roman Church 197
    Compare / Contrast: Adam & Christ 199
    Glossary 200

> As we *pour our hearts* into the study of the book of Romans, we will be *transformed* by God's grace and be *overwhelmed* by His abundant mercy to us.

WEEK 1 - DAY 1

THIS IS THE GOSPEL
Read Romans 1-16

Romans is the gospel. It is sixteen chapters of gospel truth. It is hard to imagine that any book of Scripture has impacted the world so much as the book of Romans. Theologians have examined it. Preachers have proclaimed it. Sinners have been transformed by it. So why should we study Romans? We should study Romans because it is the words of God. We should study Romans because it is the gospel. We should study Romans because it will transform us.

The book of Romans holds an important place in church history. From Augustine to Calvin, history is full of Christians that have gone before us and proclaimed the treasure of this book. Many of them asserted that Romans is the key to understanding the entire Bible. Martin Luther said of Romans:

> *"This epistle is the chief part of the New Testament and the very purest gospel, which indeed deserves that a Christian should not only know it word for word by heart, but deal with it daily as with the daily bread of the soul, for it can never be read or considered too much or too well, and the more it is handled the more delightful it becomes and the better it tastes."*

The book of Romans is a letter, or an epistle. It was written by Paul to believers in Rome that were both Jew and Gentile, and it is believed to have been written from Corinth. The book is full of quotations and allusions to the Old Testament. Paul was a Jew who was also a Roman citizen, so he was uniquely equipped by God to deliver this message at this exact time. It is estimated to have been written in approximately 56-57 AD. Written during a time period in which Rome was the center of the world, it proclaims the power of the gospel, justification by faith, and the life of the new covenant people of God.

Romans sets forth Christ as supreme and the answer to our sin and depravity. Paul exquisitely shows us the beauty of grace and the magnitude of God's holiness. It explains to us that we are justified by faith. It helps us to understand the eternal plan and purpose of God for His people. It skillfully details for us what the Christian life should look like, and it points us forward to our future hope. The book of Romans is the gospel.

As we pour our hearts into the study of the book of Romans, we will be transformed by God's grace and be overwhelmed by His abundant mercy to us. We will weep in repentance over our sinful condition, and we will rejoice in the cross. We will be moved to worship and compelled to adoration and thanksgiving. Our hearts will be centered on the gospel and left in awe of God's sovereign grace.

As you read the entire book of Romans, note any key themes, words, or concepts and mark them below.

2 *Romans 1:16-17* are the key verses of the book of Romans. Paraphrase them below.

3 Summarize the *message* of the book of Romans below in just a few sentences.

Paul, a servant of Christ Jesus, called as an apostle and set apart for the gospel of God

ROMANS 1:1

WEEK 1 - DAY 2

THE MESSENGER

Read Romans 1:1

Romans is a letter. And as was customary at the time, a letter begins with some information about the author. So, in this first verse of Romans, Paul lets us know a little bit about himself. We could easily brush right over the words of this introduction, but they hold valuable truths for us that we must grasp as we set out on our journey through the book of Romans.

Paul will introduce himself to us with three statements, and each one builds on the last and gives us a fuller picture of who Paul is and why he is writing this letter. The first thing that Paul tells us is that he is a servant of Christ Jesus. The word here used for "servant" is the Greek word *doulos* and could be literally translated as "slave" or "bond-servant." The concept would have been familiar to Paul's readers, and later Paul will expound upon this message by telling us that as believers we are no longer slaves to sin but are now slaves to righteousness (Romans 6:15-23). The irony of these words coming from Paul is that in a time in history when the vast majority of people were slaves, Paul was actually born as a free man, and yet he was so compelled by the love of Christ that he voluntarily called himself a slave to Christ. Paul had come face to face with his own sin and the glorious gospel and was compelled to submit himself to Christ and to proclaim the message of salvation.

Paul also tells us that he is called to be an apostle. The word "apostle" literally means "sent one," and that is exactly what Paul was. The office of apostle was an important role in the early church. These men spoke and wrote with the authority of God as His delegates or representatives. They had been called by God for a specific purpose and a specific point in time. One of the qualifications of an apostle that is noted in the Scriptures is the need to have seen the resurrected Christ. At first glance, Paul does not seem to meet the qualifications, but in 1 Corinthians 15:1-11, Paul speaks to this as he talks of the resurrection. He tells us here that after appearing to the apostles and many others, that Christ had appeared to him. Paul who had once been an enemy of God and had persecuted the church had seen Jesus on the road to Damascus (Acts 9). Paul writes these words as an apostle, and the weight of this must not be lost on us. Paul writes these words with the authority of God. The words of Paul in the book of Romans are the very words of God to us.

In his last descriptive statement, Paul gives us a glimpse into not only his identity and his vocation, but also to his purpose and the theme of this book. Paul has been set apart for the gospel of God. He has been chosen for this task of preaching the good

news of Jesus before he was born (Galatians 1:1, 15-16). God in His sovereignty had chosen Paul to be the one to bring this message and many others in our New Testament. He had chosen one who seemed like an unlikely candidate but was actually the perfect one to deliver this message. From the eyes of the world, Paul seemed like a bad choice. He had once persecuted and even murdered Christians. But God knew that he would be the best person to declare this message. Paul was intimately acquainted with his great need, and he held a unique social position as a Jew who was also a Roman citizen. He had the unique opportunity to reach both Jews and Gentiles. Paul was set apart by God to preach the gospel and to write the book of Romans, and God in His sovereignty has placed us in this moment in time and allowed us to open up this epistle and read it today. Just as God called Paul for a unique purpose, He has called each of His children for a unique purpose and placed us exactly where we need to be to serve Him.

As we read these three statements that Paul uses to describe himself, may we be encouraged to view ourselves not in light of our own accomplishments and accolades, but in light of who God is. Even when speaking of himself, Paul is not speaking of himself. Instead he is pointing to the one who is so much greater than himself. May we speak and live in a way that points to Christ.

Paul had come face to face with *his own sin* and the *glorious gospel* and was compelled to submit himself to Christ and to proclaim the *message of salvation.*

1. Paul uses *three phrases* to describe himself. Write them below.

2. What three phrases would you use to describe *yourself*?

3. Paul says that he is called and set apart. Read *Galatians 1:15-16* to read more about Paul's perspective on his calling. You can also read *Jeremiah 1:5*. How do these passages grow your understanding about how God calls His people?

4. How does *God's sovereignty* (His supreme power and authority) enable us to trust Him?

> The *message* of the gospel plunges to the depths of our hearts with His *overflowing grace.*

WEEK 1 - DAY 3

THE GOSPEL IS JESUS

Read Romans 1:1-6

What is the gospel? We have already learned that the message of the book of Romans is the gospel, but what exactly is it? Paul makes sure to start this letter by telling us just that. In these short verses, he gives us a condensed overview of what the gospel is, and then he will go on to explain it in detail through the whole book of Romans.

The first thing that he tells us about this gospel is that it is not new. In fact, it is very old. Paul tells us that it was promised through the prophets in Scripture. We have said that the theme of the book of Romans is the gospel, but in fact the theme of the entire Bible is the gospel. The Scriptures proclaim the gospel of Jesus on every page. From the first promise of the Messiah and the first mention of the gospel in Genesis 3:15, Scripture has been pointing toward Jesus. From the promises to Abraham (Genesis 12,15,17) to the covenant with David (2 Samuel 7), Scripture has been proclaiming the One who would change everything. The patriarchs waited for Him, the prophets proclaimed Him, and God sent Him. Now He has been revealed to us, and we will never be the same.

What is this gospel? This good news? The gospel is Jesus. The good news is Jesus. And there is no good news without Him. Without Him we would be lost and helpless, but Jesus has changed everything.

The gospel is that though we were weak and sinful, God sent Jesus to rescue us. Jesus came as the promised Son of David. Though He had always been, He came through the line of David, born of a virgin. He took on flesh. He became a man. He faced the things that we face and suffered in ways that we could never imagine. He came humbly as a servant.

Though He came as a humble servant and suffered and died for our sin, He also rose from the dead. He defeated death and conquered the grave. And His resurrection declared that not only was He the humble Son of Man, but He was also the all-powerful Son of God. Jesus Christ is the Lord. He is our Lord. The Humble Servant is also the Exalted King.

It is through Jesus that we receive grace. The message of the gospel plunges to the depths of our hearts with His overflowing grace. The gospel is Jesus, and salvation is Jesus. Paul grounds us in Christology from the start of this book. We will never understand the beauty of the gospel and the message of salvation apart from the One that they center upon.

The amazing thing about the grace that we receive through Jesus is that it compels us to action. The gospel is active. Salvation that is by faith alone through grace alone leads us to obey. It transforms not just our outward actions, but our inward thoughts and motivations. It transforms us from the inside out.

It compels us to obedience, and it compels us to spread this message to the nations. In essence, Paul is saying that if this message of the gospel is true (and it is), then it is going to change everything—and we will be compelled to share it. We share it not for our own glory, but for the sake of His name. We live to the glory of God.

As His children we have been called to belong to Jesus. This message of the gospel has been declared through the Scriptures and has been the definite plan of God since before the foundation of the world (Acts 2:23-24, 1 Peter 1:18-21), and in that same way we have been called to belong to Christ before the foundation of the world (Ephesians 1:4-10). We who were once outcasts and far from God have been called to belong. Called to be His own. Is there any greater comfort than to see the glorious grace of the gospel of Jesus and then to know that we have been called to belong to Him?

As His children we have been called to *belong to Jesus*

1. Paraphrase *Romans 1:2-6* in your own words.

2. What is the *gospel?*

3. How should the humility of Jesus' life and the triumph of the resurrection change *the way that we live?*

4. How do you *find comfort* in the fact that we are called to belong to Jesus? Have you ever felt like you didn't belong? How does that give deeper meaning to what it means to belong to Jesus?

To all who are in Rome, *loved by God, called as saints*. Grace to you and peace from God our Father and the Lord Jesus Christ.

ROMANS 1:7

WEEK 1 - DAY 4

LOVED. CALLED. SAINTS.

Read Romans 1:7

It would seem that right in the middle of his introduction Paul was so overwhelmed with the gospel that he had to pause to share it with us. In this verse he resumes his greetings, and yet here again we find the message of gospel-hope infused in every word. Paul addresses and describes his audience in Rome, but as we look closer at this opening greeting we can see that these words are applicable to every person who has been redeemed by the grace of God.

Paul had just spoken of his audience in verse 6 as those who have been called to belong to Jesus. As he moves into verse 7 he speaks of those in Rome who are loved by God and called to be saints. We could easily skim past this greeting, but the depth that is found here should not be missed by us as we read.

Remember these words are descriptive of not just the Roman Christians, but of us as well. This short verse is identity-shifting for us. He begins by calling them loved of God. We are the beloved of God, His precious children. Grasping the magnificent truth that we are loved by God is essential to a right understanding of the gospel. We must take notice that the focus here is on God loving us and not us loving God. We are so tempted to think that our identity depends on us, but Paul makes it clear that it depends solely on who God is and what He has done. We have become so accustomed to the notion that God loves us that it is easy for us not to feel the weight and glory of those words. We are loved by God. You are loved by God. Not because of anything wonderful that you have done, but simply because He has set His love on you. This is the initiating love of God. We were running in the opposite direction, and He pursued us.

Perhaps one of the greatest descriptions of this love is found in another one of Paul's letters. In Ephesians 2:1-5, Paul reminds us that we were dead in our trespasses and sins. Then in verse 4 he shows us the thing that changed us from what we were to what we now are. The verse starts with two little words that change everything, But God. God in His overflowing mercy and grace loved us with a love so great it is beyond comprehension, and He took those who were once dead and made us alive in Christ. The same word that appears here in Romans and is translated as "loved" or "beloved" also appears in Matthew 3:17 at the baptism of Jesus. Here we are told that God the Father looked down and said that Jesus was His Beloved Son. Think about that. The way that God looks at Jesus is the way that He looks at us. Through union with Christ we are able to be called the beloved of God. He has set His affection on us and called us His own.

The next word used to describe the people of God is "called." The word is the same one that appeared back in verse 1 where we saw that Paul was called to be an apostle. He was chosen by God to fulfill that role, and the same is true of us. We have been called, chosen, and set apart to be the children of God. The descriptors of these verses echo the way that the nation of Israel was described in the Old Testament. Paul is making a point that as God's children we are now a part of the people of God.

We see that we are called to be saints. The word "saints" does not refer to some super-spiritual group of believers, but instead it is used of all believers. The word "saint" means "holy one" or "set apart." In essence, the phrase "called to be saints" could be translated as "set apart to be set apart ones." We are God's people called to holiness. In one sense this calling of holiness is something that we already have positionally in Christ, and in another way, it is also something that we are constantly growing toward through the process of sanctification.

The verse closes with the greeting of grace and peace. The words echo the Aaronic blessing of Numbers 6:25-26 and sum up all that God has done for His people. Through Him we receive grace, and because of that grace we live in peace.

This verse is a description of our identity. It tells us who we are. And in telling us who we are, it tells us who God is. Because everything we are is tied to everything He is. The gospel is not about what we do, it is about what God has done for us. We are loved, called, saints. We are His. May that truth sink into our hearts and transform every part of how we live.

> **Everything we are is tied to *everything He is***

1 How should an understanding of *our identity* change the way that we live?

2 Read *Ephesians 2:1-5* and think about how these verses deepen your understanding of what God has done for us. Paraphrase the verses below.

3 How is the *description of believers* in verse 7 made possible by the gospel that Paul described in verses 1-6?

4 How does the fact that *the gospel is not about what we do but about what Jesus has done for us* enable us to live freely?

> First, I *thank my God* through Jesus Christ for all of you because the *news of your faith* is being reported in all the world.
>
> ROMANS 1:8

WEEK 1 - DAY 5

I THANK MY GOD

Read Romans 1:8-15

Paul continues his introduction by sharing his heart with the Christians in Rome. His words give us insight into how Jesus should transform our relationship to other people and our response to God and our own dreams and goals.

Paul begins by telling the believers in Rome that he thanks His God through Jesus for them. Again, Paul is bringing us back to the gospel and reminding us that God is personal. He is "my" God because of what Jesus has done on the cross. And it is through Jesus that we are boldly able to approach the throne of God in prayer (Hebrews 10:19). Because of Jesus we can come to God with confidence. Paul not only thanks these believers whose faith was spreading around the world, but he also prays for them. He prays for these Christians that he has never even met. Not only does he pray for them, but the text tells us that he is always praying for them. Paul is reminding us that we should not only pray self-centered prayers, but also pray for our brothers and sisters around the world.

Paul could have been jealous of what God was doing in Rome. We know that Paul desired to go to Rome and be a part of the work that was happening there. Though he was not able to do that, we do not see him competing with this church or being jealous of what God was doing through their ministry. Instead, we see Paul praying for them and thanking God for them.

Paul tells them that he desires to come to them and strengthen them through the Word of God. Yet he also recognizes that part of being of the people of God is that as believers we mutually encourage each other. Paul was an apostle and an incredible encourager, but he also needed to be encouraged by other believers. We are made for Christian community. We are made for the church. We are not meant to journey through this life alone but instead to encourage one another to pursue Jesus.

Paul wanted to go to see them, but he tells us that he has been prevented from doing so. His desire was to go and preach the gospel there in order to strengthen their faith. He desired to also see people converted by the power of the gospel. He recognized that as one who had experienced the grace of God, he was indebted to share the message of Jesus with everyone that he could. Though Paul had been prevented up until this point in coming to Rome to encourage the Christians there, he was able to write this letter to them. Perhaps it is a gift of grace to us that Paul was prevented at first so that we would be able to read the words of the book of Romans.

Paul wanted to go to Rome, but only if it was God's will for him to do so. This is a valuable lesson for us to learn to submit our own wishes, dreams, plans, and desires to the sovereign hand of God. God always does what is best, and if He is closing a door that we would like to be open, we can trust that it is for our good. Even the great apostle Paul had desires that needed to be submitted to God. The God of the gospel is also the God of our days. He will do what is best for us and will use every situation for our good.

Paul would eventually arrive in Rome, though likely not in the way that he was hoping or anticipating. Acts 28 tells us that Paul arrived in Rome in chains as a prisoner. Church history tells us that it would be in Rome that Paul would be martyred for his faith in Jesus.

In these short verses, we are reminded of our need for other believers and the way that we should relate to them. We are made to encourage and exhort each other. We are made to pray for and be thankful for each other. And this is all made possible because of what Jesus has done for us. The gospel brings us into relationship with God, and also into relationship with other believers. And it is a joy to serve Jesus with each other.

> We are not meant to journey through this life alone but instead to *encourage one another* to pursue Jesus.

1 Look back at the passage and record the things that Paul did in regard to the believers in Rome. How does this transform your understanding of the *relationship between believers*?

2 Think back to a time when another believer encouraged you in your faith. How can you *encourage other believers*?

3 How does the *beauty of the gospel* compel us to share it with others? How can you share the gospel message with others?

4 In what areas of your life do you need to *submit* your own plans, desires, goals, and dreams to the will of God?

ROMANS 8:1-3

Therefore, there is now *no condemnation* for those in Christ Jesus, because the law of the Spirit of life in Christ Jesus has *set you free from the law of sin and death.* What the law could not do since it was weakened by the flesh, *God did.* He condemned sin in the flesh by sending his own Son in the likeness of sinful flesh as a sin offering

WEEK 1 MEMORY VERSE

WEEK ONE *Reflection*

READ ROMANS 1:1-15

Paraphrase the passage from this week.

What did you observe from this week's text about God and His character?

What does the passage teach about the condition of mankind and about yourself?

How does this passage point to the gospel?

How should you respond to this passage? What is the personal application?

What specific action steps can you take this week to apply the passage?

> The gospel *is* everything, and it *changes* everything.

WEEK 2 - DAY 1

THE GOSPEL IS EVERYTHING

Read Romans 1:16-17

The gospel is everything. Paul has introduced us to himself, to the gospel, and to his purpose in writing this book. Now he ends his introduction of the book with his thesis statement. This is the theme of the book of Romans encapsulated in two verses. These two short verses describe the magnificent truth of the gospel. It is these two verses that opened the eyes of Martin Luther to the beauty of salvation by grace alone through faith alone. It is in these two verses that countless others have been led to come to Jesus. And these two verses hold rich truth and comfort overflowing with gospel-hope for us.

Paul begins a new thought with the word "for" that also connects it back to what he has just written. He has just told us that he is eager to preach the gospel, and now he states a similar point in the negative. He tells us that he is not ashamed of the gospel. This is the position that our hearts should be in as well. It is easy for us to skim these words and assure ourselves that we are not ashamed of the gospel, but we must pause for a moment here. Paul states that he is not ashamed of the gospel, because he knows that our tendency is often to be ashamed of the gospel. Being ashamed of the gospel is something that can pop up in our hearts in many ways, and it is something that we must actively fight against. Instead of being unsure what to say when people ask about our faith, church, or Bible study, we can proclaim the good news with joy and boldness. There will be those that do not agree and there will be those that reject the gospel, but we must continue to proclaim this good news.

Jesus spoke to His disciples about not being ashamed of the gospel (Mark 8:34-38), and Paul would reiterate similar themes to the Corinthians and to Timothy (1 Corinthians 1:18-25, 2 Timothy 1:8,12). To the world, the gospel sounds like foolishness, but we know that the cross has changed everything. The power of the gospel in my own life drives away feelings of shame and timidity and instills in my heart boldness to proclaim the truth. The word "gospel" is the Greek *euaggelion* and literally means "good news." The gospel is the message of the good news of Jesus. It is the message of creation-fall-redemption-restoration. It is the message that God created us to be His people in perfect communion with Him. It is the message that at the fall sin came into the world and destroyed that communion. It is the message that Jesus came and lived the perfect life that we could not live and died the death that we deserved, and that through Jesus and His sacrificial death on the cross, salvation is freely offered to all. It is the message that for the people of God there is coming a day when all

will be restored, and we will dwell in full and perfect communion with our God once again. The message of the gospel brings hope to the weary and healing to the broken.

We are not ashamed of the gospel because it is the power of God. The gospel is the way that God brings about salvation. The gospel is steadfast and sure. The gospel is our enduring hope. The gospel is the power of God, and God will never fail. We can trust Him to do what He has said that He will do. He has told us that the gospel saves, and we can have ultimate confidence that there is nothing that will separate us from the love of God. Paul speaks more about this in Romans 8:29-39. We are told about the work of salvation that God has accomplished, and then we are reminded that because God has done this for us there is nothing that can separate us from the overflowing, abundant, pursuing, initiating love of God. Martyn Lloyd-Jones wrote, "Let everything on earth and in hell do its utmost to thwart God's purpose and oppose His power, and it is certain to fail." This is the confidence we have in God's accomplishing power. No plan or scheme of those on earth or those in hell will ever prevent the perfect plan of God.

The gospel is the power of God for salvation for everyone who believes. Salvation is not just a concept; it is something that God does for us. It is not about what we do, but about what He so graciously has done for us. It is for every person that believes. It is extended to every person. It is extended first to the Jews as we see historically referring to the gospel coming through the Hebrew people who were the first covenant people of God. And then it is extended to Greeks or Gentiles, and this is a reference to the rest of the world. The gospel is the power of God for salvation to every person from any tribe, tongue, and nation that will believe.

The gospel is the good news. It is the best news that has ever been. The gospel is a person. The gospel is Jesus. And the gospel should move us to worship because of all that God has done for us through Jesus. The gospel is everything, and it changes everything.

1. Paraphrase *Romans 1:16.* Does this paraphrase differ from the paraphrase you wrote on Week 1, Day 1? If so, how?

2. Can you think of a time you have felt *ashamed* or have been *tempted* to not share the gospel?

3. What would it look like to be *not ashamed* of the gospel?

4. How does the truth that the gospel is the *power of God for salvation* bring you hope?

For in it the righteousness of God is revealed from faith to faith, just as it is written: *The righteous will live by faith.*

ROMANS 1:17

WEEK 2 - DAY 2

THE RIGHTEOUS SHALL LIVE BY FAITH

Read Romans 1:16-17

We come again to these pivotal two verses. They are full of rich theology and practical truth for us. In verse 16, we were exhorted by Paul's declaration that he is not ashamed of the gospel. And then we were encouraged with the truth that the gospel is the power of God that brings about salvation to all who believe. Here in verse 17, we see that the gospel is the power of God for salvation because in it the righteousness of God is revealed.

We must think about what it means that the righteousness of God is revealed through the gospel. There are several aspects of the righteousness of God, and they are all brought together in the gospel. The righteousness of God in one sense is who He is. It is part of His character and one of His attributes. Our God is righteous. He is perfectly just and faithful (Psalm 145:17, Isaiah 45:21). He only does what is good, and He is a covenant-keeping God. The righteousness of God is also something that God does. Everything God does is righteous and holy. The term "righteousness" is also used to describe God's saving work. The salvation of God's people is often described as God's righteousness, specifically in the Psalms and Isaiah (Psalm 71:2, Psalm 98:2, Isaiah 46:13, Isaiah 51:5). Finally, the righteousness of God is the status that He gives to His people. Salvation is the great exchange where God takes our sin and declares us to be righteous. Because of our union with Christ we are declared to be righteous before God (2 Corinthians 5:21). What is the righteousness of God? It is all of these things. Righteousness is who God is, what He does, and what He has given us. Righteousness comes only through the gospel and the gospel comes only through Jesus.

This beautiful and complete righteousness is revealed or made known through the gospel. Verse 17 tells us that it is revealed from faith for faith or from faith to faith. Paul seems to be emphasizing the supremacy of faith. Faith is the conduit through which we receive the grace of the gospel. It is from faith in God's grace that it is received, and it is for the purpose of living a life of faith. We are saved by grace through faith (Ephesians 2:8-9), and we also live by grace through faith.

Paul then quotes from Habakkuk 2:4 when he says that the righteous shall live by faith. These six short words encompass some of the most life-changing and transformative truths of the gospel. The truth that is being set forth for us here is that those that have been made righteous by God through faith in the gospel shall live eternally. We are righteous not by any merit of our own, but by faith in Jesus

and His saving work on the cross. Many scholars have said that this verse could also be translated as, "the righteous by faith shall live." So, this verse is not simply about living a life of faith but being made righteous through our faith and being made alive together with Christ (Ephesians 2:5-10). We are made alive not by our own merit, but because of God's sure and certain power of salvation in making us righteous. We have eternal life because we have been made righteous by faith.

May we never be ashamed of the beauty of the gospel. The gospel is everything to us. It is God's power to bring about salvation to every person from every nation that will believe. The gospel declares the righteous character and work of Christ, and through the gospel God declares that we are made righteous. In salvation, not only are our sins washed white as snow, but we are given the righteousness of God. We are made righteous by faith in the saving work of Jesus and because of that salvation we are made alive. We have union with Christ because of the cross.

Our salvation is by grace alone through faith alone. We rest our hearts in the power of the gospel.

> Our salvation is by *grace alone* through *faith alone*. We rest our hearts in the power of the gospel.

1. Write out yesterday's paraphrase of *Romans 1:16* and add a paraphrase of *Romans 1:17*. Does this paraphrase differ from the paraphrase you wrote on Week 1, Day 1? If so, how?

2. What is the *righteousness of God*?

3. How is the *righteousness of God* revealed to us in the gospel?

4. Read *Ephesians 2:5-10*. What things do people sometimes think they must do to earn salvation? What does this passage tell us about salvation?

> We need a Savior because *we are incapable* of saving ourselves.

WEEK 2 – DAY 3

THE WRATH OF GOD REVEALED

Read Romans 1:18-23

In order for us to understand the good news of the gospel, we must first understand why it is good news. So, in Romans 1:18-3:20, Paul stops to tell us why the truth of salvation through faith in God's grace is good news. Why do we need the righteousness of God? Why do we need to be justified before God?

In verse 17, we were told that the righteousness of God is revealed from faith to faith. Now here in verse 18, we see that the wrath of God is revealed against ungodliness and unrighteousness. Wrath is not always something that we like to talk about. It is important to note that the wrath of God is not what we think of when we think of human wrath. It is not uncontrolled anger, but instead it is controlled opposition to sin and evil. God in His holiness cannot even look on sin. He hates sin and all the evil that it brings about. The wrath of God motivated Paul to share the message of the gospel. Humanity has a problem, and when we understand the problem, we are not only moved to repentance for ourselves, but also compelled to tell others that despite the wrath of God against ungodliness, there is hope in the gospel. God's wrath is revealed to us at the cross where Jesus paid the price for our sin and bore the wrath of God in our place. The wrath of God is satisfied at the cross, and the love of God is displayed at the cross. The wrath of God and the love of God are not opposed to each other; instead they come together in the work of Christ to pay for our salvation.

The question of why we need to be saved by grace through faith is revealed here in these verses. We need a Savior because we are incapable of saving ourselves. We are utterly hopeless without Jesus. In unrighteousness those that have not been converted suppress the truth of the gospel by trying to ignore it and live as if it doesn't exist. People reject Jesus because they do not think that they need Him. Even as believers we can be tempted to live as if we do not need the Lord. Jesus reminded the religious leaders that it is only the sick that need a physician (Mark 2:17). The news of our condition apart from Christ is bad news, but it makes our hearts yearn for the good news of the gospel.

Paul goes on to explain how every person in the world is without excuse and guilty before God for their sin. Every person can look at the world and see that there is a God. Psalm 19 tells us that the heavens declare His glory. All of earth points to the glory and majesty of God. The intricacies of the world declare that there is a God and that He has created this world. Humanity points to the One in whose image we are made. Verse 20 tells us that the world displays for us the invisible attributes of God. The invisible is made visible through His handiwork. This general revelation of God leaves

all of humanity without excuse for their ungodliness and unrighteousness. Though the revelation of God through nature has no power to save, it points all people to their need for a Savior.

The following verses speak to what happens when people know of God and choose to suppress the truth. They do not honor Him as God, and they do not recognize that all they have comes from Him. Their thinking is futile, foolish, or worthless. Their foolish and wicked hearts are darkened by their suppression of the truth. They think they are wise, perhaps mocking those that place their faith in Christ, and yet in their rejection of the gospel that they view as wisdom they have proven that they are fools. Instead of worshiping the God that has sacrificed His own Son for salvation, they reject the hope of the gospel. They worship other things instead of worshiping God. They exchange the worship of God for the worship of things that will never bring joy or hope. All sin is a worship problem. When we worship other things, people, and even ourselves we make idols out of things that will never fulfill the longings of our hearts. We exchange eternal hope for momentary pleasure, and that only ever leads to emptiness.

There is another exchange that is worth us turning our gaze to. The great exchange is that at the cross Jesus bore the wrath of God for our sin. And in exchange for the sin that once weighed us down, we are given the imputed righteousness of God. Though we could do nothing to earn it, God lavished it upon us as a gift of His magnificent grace, and He offers it to all who will believe. This is the gospel. The wrath of God is heavy, but Jesus bore that wrath for His children. This is why we can say that the righteous will live by faith, because Jesus has made us righteous.

1. Why do we need to understand the *wrath of God* to understand the gospel?

2. How does the cross reveal the *wrath of God*?

3. What do we learn in *creation* about God?

4. How should the *message of the wrath of God* compel us to share the gospel?

Although *they know God's just sentence* — that those who practice such things deserve to die — they not only do them, but even applaud others who practice them.

ROMANS 1:32

WEEK 2 - DAY 4

THE DEPRAVITY OF HUMANITY

Read Romans 1:24-32

The words of today's reading from Romans are heavy. The verses that we examine today show us the depths of the depravity of man and cause us as believers to rejoice in the hope of the gospel.

The condition of humanity without God is bleak and hopeless. In these verses, Paul continues to speak about the state of men and women without Christ. We again are drawn to the truth that everyone worships something. All sin is a worship problem. Though there are many that will refuse to worship God or even acknowledge Him, they replace the worship that should be given to God with worship of some other thing or person. Humans are worshipers. We all attribute praise and honor to something. We all have something in our lives that is the most important thing to us. Worship should however be reserved for God alone, but sadly this is not always the case. Even believers are tempted to worship things that are not God. We worship our relationships, families, jobs, hobbies, and even our own intellect. This shows up in many ways. It reveals itself through how we spend our time and what we think about most. It reveals itself through what makes us sad and what makes us happy. It is even revealed through how we spend our money. We must constantly be refocusing our hearts and going back to Scripture to realign our hearts with the truth and worship God alone.

Three times throughout these few short verses, we see the phrase that God "gave them up." I am not sure if there are any more sobering words in all of Scripture. These verses paint for us a picture of humanity that has so rejected God and turned to the temporary pleasures of sin, that God gives them up to partake in that sin and all of its consequences. We can be assured that sin will never satisfy. Sin may seem to satisfy us for a moment, but the end result is always emptiness, brokenness, and death. But the hope of Jesus breaks through the darkness of sin and gives fullness, healing, and life. Sin never satisfies, but Jesus always does.

The amount of different types of sin that are enumerated in these verses is staggering. But Paul is making his case for why we need Jesus. One look at these verses should remind us of our own desperate need for salvation and compel us to share this gospel with a world that is in need of Jesus. Paul speaks of lust and impurity and fixes our focus on the devastating impact of sexual sin. The Bible is a love story. It is a grand story of redemption. Earthly marriage is an illustration of the beauty of the gospel, so it is no wonder that so often marriage and sexuality are one of the first things to be attacked by the culture. When we exchange the worship of God for the worship of ourselves, sin quickly follows. Our enemy knows that sexuality is

a battleground. What was made for our pleasure has been transformed by sin to destroy us. Paul speaks both generally of impurity that dishonors our bodies, and specifically of homosexual sin. Sexual sin takes what is natural, referring to the way God created it to be, and changes it into something that is unnatural and against God's created order. Sexuality apart from God's design of a man and woman in the confines of covenant marriage is against God's design. The penalty for sin is not just the wrath of God that was observed in earlier verses, but the sin itself is also the penalty. Living in the sin that never satisfies is a consequence of choosing sin over God.

Paul begins with sexual sin as his example and then moves onto a much broader list. It is as if Paul is setting forth an example of our depravity and then listing out at least twenty-one other sins and categories of sins that display our depravity as well. Paul wants to make us abundantly aware that sin is not just a problem of a select few that struggle with one certain kind of sin, but that the problem of depravity is widespread and all-encompassing. Humanity is filled with unrighteousness, evil, greed, wickedness, envy, murder, quarrels, deceit, malice, gossip, slander, haters of God, arrogance, pride, boasting, inventors of evil, disobedience, foolishness, untrustworthiness, heartlessness, and ruthlessness. No one is outside of the reach of the sin that he describes. This is the human condition apart from grace.

Today's reading was weighty. But now go back and read Romans 1:16-17 again. The depth of our depravity is deep. The weight of our sin is heavy. But there is an answer to the crushing weight of our sin. It is found in the one who bore that sin for us. It is found in the one who was crushed for us. Hope is found in Jesus who bore the penalty for our sin fully and completely. We can rejoice when we see the weight of our sin and are reminded that when God looks at His children, He no longer sees our unrighteousness, but instead sees the righteousness of Christ that we have been clothed in. The filth of our sin has been washed white as snow with the blood of the Lamb. That should make us turn our hearts to adoration and lift our voices in praise. There is hope for sinners, and His name is Jesus.

1. What are some things that people worship other than God?

2. What about you? What do you sometimes worship and prioritize instead of God? What are the idols of your heart?

3. Read John 3:18. There is condemnation of sin apart from Christ, but what does this verse tell us that is true of us if we are a believer?

4. How does the depth of the depravity of man magnify the truth of the gospel set forth in Romans 1:16-17?

> The *good news* of the gospel begins with a *deep understanding* of the depravity of our condition.

WEEK 2 - DAY 5

LEAD US TO REPENTANCE

Read Romans 2:1-4

We see sin in everyone but ourselves. This is the message that is brought to us in these short verses. Our temptation is to read the end of chapter one and see the desperate state of humanity and to think of it as the state of other people. But lest we read those heavy words and think that they do not apply to us, Paul continues his letter before the thought can even enter our hearts. He reveals for us in these verses the plague of hypocrisy that inflicts us.

This message is first for those that are not believers but think that they are good people. These are those that think that while the world has some terrible things that take place in it, the majority of humanity is basically good. This however is not the message of the gospel. The good news of the gospel begins with a deep understanding of the depravity of our condition. We are not only far from God and lost in sin, we are so far that we look at our sin and think it isn't that bad. Our problem is that we are measuring ourselves against the wrong standard. When we measure ourselves against the standard of other people, we will always be able to find someone that we think we are better than. But when we measure ourselves against God, we realize that we fall woefully short. This is why we need the gospel.

Paul specifically speaks to those who judge others. He speaks to those who read Romans 1 and think it is not speaking to their own condition. He speaks to those who think that they have a right relationship with God because they do Christian things. He reminds us that God is concerned with our hearts and not just our outward appearance. It is reminiscent of the lessons that Jesus taught in the Sermon on the Mount (Matthew 5-7), and of the parable that Jesus taught of the Pharisee and the tax collector (Luke 18:9-14). Jesus stunned those that listened when He declared that the one that was justified was the tax collector. God is not looking for the outwardly religious but for hearts transformed by grace. But Paul points out how deep this problem goes. Not only do some judge others for their sin; the same people are committing the same kinds of sin in secret. They think their own lust is not a big deal while they condemn the one in adultery. They live in disdain of those that worship idols while they build idols of materialism and relationships in their hearts. They criticize the sin of others while harboring the same sins in their own hearts. This is us. This is what we do. This is how we live. We listen to a sermon and think about how so-and-so really needed to hear it. We become frustrated with a friend or our spouse when they sin against us in the same way that we sin against them and others. We are frustrated with our children for the same things that we do against our heavenly Father.

The problem in these verses is not speaking out against sin, because we are called to be a light in this world. The problem is judging others for the things that we ourselves are doing. The problem is thinking that God should punish others and give leniency to us. We insult God's magnificent grace when we take our own sin lightly. 2 Samuel 12 is a wonderful illustration of this for us. After David had slept with Bathsheba and conceived a child with her, he then had her husband murdered. He had abused his power, and his sin had led him down a slippery slope. The prophet Nathan confronted David about his sin in this chapter by telling him a story about a man who had taken the lamb of another man. David was enraged by the story that he heard and demanded justice, only for Nathan to point out to him that he was the man. This illustrates for us the tendency to view the sin of others as worse than our own just as David did.

The verses that end this passage in no way are teaching that salvation can come by works. That goes against all that Paul has been teaching about justification through faith (Romans 1:16-17). Paul is instead reminding us that the fruit of our lives reveals the presence of God in our lives. We are not saved by our works, but our works reveal our salvation (James 2:18). Paul speaks these words in contrast to the warning against hypocrisy at the start of the passage. The works that reveal our salvation are not the works of hypocrisy where we try to make other people think we have it all together or works that are done in our own strength. Instead the believer bears the fruit of the Spirit (Galatians 5:22-23). God is a just and impartial judge. For those that reject Christ there is judgement, and for those that place their faith in Jesus there is eternal life.

As stated in verse 4, so often our practice is to presume on the kindness of God. We see His righteous and good character, His love and His mercy, and we presume that He will be gracious and merciful to us as we continue in sin. Paul pleads here that we not do this. God's kindness is meant to lead and call us to repentance. For the unbeliever, the kindness of God is God's call to salvation. For the Christian, God's kindness is a call to holiness. Billy Graham once said, "The ground is level at the foot of the cross." As we come to the cross and see the price that Jesus paid may our hearts not be tempted to think that our sin is more acceptable than the sin of another. May we be humbled by His love and grace and brought to repentance by His unfailing love and grace.

> # Or do you despise the riches of his kindness, restraint, and patience, not recognizing that God's kindness is intended to *lead you to repentance*?
>
> ## ROMANS 2:4

1. Paul is describing *hypocrisy* for us in these verses. Look up the word "hypocrisy" and write the definition below.

2. Read *Luke 18:9-14*. In what ways can we often be like the Pharisee in this story?

3. In what areas of life are you tempted to *judge other people* for the same sins that you commit?

4. How can we find *freedom* in acknowledging our sin and need before the Lord?

ROMANS 8:4-6

in order that the law's requirement would be fulfilled in us who do not walk according to the flesh but according to the Spirit. For those who live according to the flesh have their minds set on the things of the flesh, but those who live according to the Spirit have their minds set on the things of the Spirit. Now the mind-set of the flesh is death, but the mind-set of the Spirit is life and peace.

WEEK 2 MEMORY VERSE

READ ROMANS 1:16 – 2:4

Paraphrase the passage from this week.

What did you observe from this week's text about God and His character?

What does the passage teach about the condition of mankind and about yourself?

How does this passage point to the gospel?

How should you respond to this passage? What is the personal application?

What specific action steps can you take this week to apply the passage?

> We need the *perfect Word of God* to be the standard to which we measure every thought and emotion.

WEEK 3 - DAY 1

THE RIGHTEOUS JUDGE

Read Romans 2:12-16

We need the gospel. We need the justification that comes through faith in the finished work of Jesus. We are hopeless without Him who is our Hope. In these verses, Paul continues to make his case for the need for salvation by faith. Paul knew that there would be some who would think that they could earn salvation on their own. He knew that there would be people that considered themselves to be religious and thought that their religion was enough. Specifically, he speaks to those that have the law and think that they are exempt from Paul's message of salvation by faith. In these verses he speaks strongly to the notion that the law has any power to save.

As a great teacher, Paul anticipates the objections that will be raised by his audience. He knows that the religious Jews will think that they have an upper hand because they have the law and Scripture. But having the law has no power in and of itself to save. Paul reminds them that they would need to keep the law perfectly, but this is not even possible. Since sin entered the world in Genesis 3, mankind has been impacted by the fall. We have no power to live up to God's perfect law. The standard of God's holiness as set forth in the law is impossible for us to meet.

But Paul also talks about those that do not know the law. He tells us here that God has written the law on their hearts and that even though they do not have the law, they know and sometimes do what the law requires. Paul is speaking here of the conscience of mankind. Even those that do not know God's Word and do not know what the law says in some ways know what is right and what is wrong. People know that murder is wrong without reading the Ten Commandments, and they know that it is wrong to steal without the revelation of Scripture. God has created us with a conscience. The conscience of man has no power to save, and it is fallible. People can sear or ignore their conscience and convince themselves that sin is ok. Verse 15 tells that the law is on their hearts and their consciences confirm this. Our minds both accuse us when we do what is wrong, and also make excuses and rationalize our sinful behavior. Our thoughts and emotions swayed by our sinful natures will try to convince us that what is bad is good and that what is good is bad, and this is why we need the perfect Word of God to be the standard to which we measure every thought and emotion. God's judgment is perfect. He sees our hearts (1 Samuel 16:7, Psalm 139:1-4, Jeremiah 17:10, Luke 16:15). He not only judges our actions, but also our motives and the secrets of our hearts as seen in verse 16.

Paul speaks of "my gospel." This is not to say that each person can make the gospel say what they

would like it to say. This is a popular concept in our culture. We think of truth as relative and talk of speaking "our truth." This is not what Paul is saying. Instead he is pointing to the fact that the gospel of God (Romans 1:1) has become his own through the power of God for salvation (Romans 1:16). Through faith, the gospel becomes our own as the blood of Christ is applied to our lives and our sins are washed away. Then we speak of the gospel not just as an abstract idea or a concept, but as a Person. The gospel is Jesus. The gospel is ours because we are in Him.

All are condemned. The one that is religious and tries to do all the right things is condemned. And the one that has never heard the gospel is condemned. We are condemned by our own sin. There is coming a day of judgement, but the hope of the gospel is that the impossible price that we could never pay has been paid for us, and we must simply accept in faith God's gift of grace. Verse 16 shows us that Jesus is the Judge, and what a comfort to believers to know that the Judge is also our Justifier. He has made us right with God and called us to Himself. The message of the wrath of God is essential to the gospel. John 3:16-18, 36 speak of the wrath of God remaining on those who do not believe, and yet they also declare that there is no condemnation for those that believe. For God's people, the message of the gospel that has changed everything for us should compel us to spread this news to everyone that we meet and to the entire world.

> The *hope of the gospel* is that the impossible price that we could never pay has been paid for us, and we must simply accept in faith God's gift of grace.

1 Paul speaks here of people thinking they would be saved because they had the law. What things do people sometimes *think* will save them?

2 Paul addresses the concept of trusting in works for salvation in *Ephesians 2:8-9*. How do these verses say that we are saved? Why are we not saved by works?

3 Read *1 Samuel 16:7, Psalm 139:1-4, Jeremiah 17:10,* and *Luke 16:15.* These verses tell us that God sees our hearts. Can you think of a time that you did the right thing, but the motives of your heart were not right?

4 How do believers find comfort in the truth that *Jesus is the Judge*?

For a person is not a Jew who is one outwardly, and *true circumcision is not something visible in the flesh*. On the contrary, a person is a Jew who is one inwardly, and *circumcision is of the heart — by the Spirit, not the letter*. That person's praise is not from people but from God.

ROMANS 2:28-29

WEEK 3 - DAY 2

A MATTER OF THE HEART
Read Romans 2:17-29

In this last section of Romans 2, Paul continues to speak of the fact that all are condemned. From the one living in sin to the one that tries to do all the right things, all humanity is condemned because no one can live up to God's holy standard of perfection. In this section, Paul speaks specifically to the religious Jews who thought that their status as a Jew meant that they did not need this gospel that Paul was preaching. But Paul is going to show them that they need it just as much an any other person that did not have the privilege that they were born with. Verse 16 reminded us that our God does not look only on the outward behavior of people but on their inward hearts. And our hearts reveal so much more than our actions ever could.

The Jews had the law, and they thought that this would be enough to justify them. After all, they were the ones that God had chosen to give the Word of God, so certainly this meant that they were justified. Paul points out the foolishness of this thought. The people had truth, and yet there was no transformation. They had the precious Word of God, and yet they failed to trust the God of the Word. Not only were they not better off because they possessed the law, they were revealing their condemnation through their hypocrisy. They spoke of the law and even taught the law, and then they did not obey it. The words of Paul here give us an allusion to the words of Jesus as He preached the Sermon on the Mount. In Matthew 5:21-6:4, Jesus spoke to many of the same issues that Paul addresses here. Jesus called to a law even higher than what had been recorded in the Old Testament to prove a point that no one can actually keep the law. This is why we need Christ, because we cannot live up to God's standard. He spoke to people that had more trust in their Jewish heritage than they did in God Himself and told them plainly that it was their hearts that needed to be changed.

Paul then moves on to his next topic. He has already told his readers that their heritage has no power to save, and now he is going to tell them that their religious rituals have no power to save. The Jewish people had the law, and they also had circumcision which was the symbol of God's covenant. If they could not depend on their possession of the law and their Jewish heritage, they certainly thought that circumcision would justify them. But Paul shines the light of truth into the darkness of religion that is based on works (Ephesians 2:8-9). Circumcision was always meant to be a symbol. In many ways it can be likened to Christian baptism. Baptism has no power to save, but instead it is meant to be a declaration that a person has been saved. It

was meant to be a visible sign of an invisible reality. It was to be a tangible picture of the spiritual. Baptism has been likened to a wedding ring, and the illustration is helpful for us to understand. Just as a wedding ring does not make a person married, baptism (or circumcision) does not make a person saved. An unmarried person can put on a wedding ring and it will not make them married. A married person can take off their wedding ring and still be married. The symbol has no power other than to declare the reality that marriage has taken place. Baptism today operates in this same way. For the Jews that were dependent on their circumcision, they had gotten the symbolism confused. But Paul is teaching them that it is not about an outward sign but an inward obedience and transformation.

Paul's words would have been shocking. His words were radical. He spoke of being a Jew inwardly, and this concept was changing the understanding of who God's people are. He declares that circumcision is a matter of the heart. This should have come as no surprise. God had spoken of having uncircumcised hearts in the Old Testament in places like Deuteronomy 30:6. And in the declaration of the new covenant that was coming, God had declared that He would give His people new hearts (Ezekiel 36:26). Paul is still focusing on the reason that we need the message of salvation, but he is also hinting at the message that is to come. This circumcision of the heart comes not by the letter or the law itself, but by the Spirit of God. The new heart of the covenant is made possible only by the God of the covenant.

Our hope is not in the temporal, but in the eternal. Our hope is not in rituals, but in the righteousness of God Himself. Our hope is not in being good enough, but in the gospel of Jesus who lived the perfect life that we could not live and died the cruel death that we deserved. We rest our faith in Jesus alone.

1 These verses reveal the *hypocrisy* of the Jews that Paul spoke to. We are all hypocrites in some ways. What areas of life is hypocrisy a temptation for you?

2 How did Jesus expand on the law in *Matthew 5:21-6:4* and point the people toward their need for Him?

3 Read *Deuteronomy 30:1-6*. What does it mean that God was going to circumcise their hearts?

4 Read *Ezekiel 36:26-27*. The law sought to govern the outward obedience of the people, but God wants us to have heart transformation. How does heart transformation lead to greater obedience?

> We are all in desperate need of the gospel.

WEEK 3 - DAY 3

THE SURPASSING FAITHFULNESS OF GOD

Read Romans 3:1-8

Paul is beginning to wrap up his case for the great need for the gospel that he has been showing us from Romans 1:18 through Romans 3:20. In this passage, he speaks to some of the arguments that the Jews will bring against this gospel message that Paul is preaching. But we will quickly see that these arguments do not stand. We are all in desperate need of the gospel. Whether Jew or Gentile, religious or non-religious, we are all in need of Jesus.

Paul presents some of the common arguments from the Jews, and then he goes on to refute them. After all that Paul said in chapter 2, the question arises—is there any advantage to being a Jew? Paul had made it clear that when it comes to salvation, there is no person that has any advantage over another. No matter what our heritage or what religious culture we have been a part of, we need the grace of God for salvation. But Paul also points out to us that that doesn't mean there were no advantages to being a Jew. One specific advantage stood above the rest. The Jews had been entrusted with the Word of God. The oracles of God had come through the Jewish people and the covenant had come from the words of God. Having the Word of God did not make all Jews justified, but it provided them with the written Word of God that pointed toward redemption and the Messiah that was to come. It was a great advantage, though it was not an advantage in salvation because all people are saved in the same way—by grace through faith. In the same way, we have access to the Word of God. May we never take it lightly that we can open a Bible and read the words of God. We have the very Word of God, and yet so often we neglect it for lesser pursuits. We choose a million other things over the living Word of God. How our lives would change if our hearts truly realized the gift of grace we have in the Scriptures.

The next objection is that if not all Jews were faithful, does that mean that God was unfaithful? Paul's response is absolutely not! Paul says that God is true though every human is a liar. Here Paul quotes from Psalm 51:4. In context, these words come from a psalm of confession from David after committing adultery with Bathsheba. David was declaring that he was a sinner in desperate need of mercy and that God was just. God's faithfulness is displayed in both His mercy and in His justice. We want God to be just. We want Him to punish the wickedness of the world, yet so often we do not want justice for our own sin. We like to speak of the fact that salvation is free. And though salvation

is free to us, it is not free. Salvation cost Jesus His life and cost God His own Son. In confession, we recognize that God is just and righteous though we are sinful and unrighteous. We acknowledge that we deserve His justice, but that for those of us that believe, the penalty of our sin has been poured out on Jesus who suffered in our place. We are unfaithful, but He is ever faithful.

The last objection is one of asking if the end justifies the means. The argument is that in sinning, and being unrighteous, humanity puts on display the righteousness of God. The argument is that somehow by being sinful, we make God look good. The argument is not only theologically incorrect, it is insulting to the character of God. God is righteous and faithful, and He does not need our sin to prove His abundant goodness. The objections that are raised may seem silly to us, but they are not uncommon. When we are confronted with our sin, our tendency is to divert the attention away from ourselves. This is true of unbelievers and should encourage us to be ready to engage them with the gospel. But it is also true of us even as believers, and it should compel us to humility before the Lord.

This passage is really a series of contrasts. God is faithful, but we are unfaithful. God is righteous, but we are unrighteous. God is the God of covenant, we are covenant breakers. And this is the point of the gospel message that Paul proclaims. We need Jesus. We need His faithfulness to cover our sin of unfaithfulness. We need His covenant-keeping love to overcome our rebellion. We need His righteousness to be our righteousness. We need the gospel, and we are transformed by it. We have all that we need because we are in Christ.

> We need His *faithfulness* to cover our sin of *unfaithfulness*.

1 Have you ever noticed how people *love to find loopholes*? This is exactly what is happening in this passage. Why do you think our human tendency is to look for loopholes?

2 In what ways does *having God's Word* come with great responsibility?

3 Have you ever felt the tendency to *divert from your own sin*? Why is it hard to confess?

4 List out a few *contrasts* between God and you. How does this lead you to worship?

as it is written:
There is no one righteous, not even one.

ROMANS 3:10

WEEK 3 - DAY 4

NO NOT ONE

Read Romans 3:9-20

Why is the gospel necessary? Why do we need Jesus? Here Paul gives us the final words of his lengthy argument about the necessity for salvation. He ends this argument that began in chapter one with a rapid-fire list of quotes from the Old Testament. He wants to prove to us once and for all our need of a once for all sacrifice. Our need is great. Our position is hopeless apart from Christ. So, Paul allows us to see the depth of our need just before he opens the flood gates so that the good news of the gospel can rush its healing waters over our soul.

These verses are a strong declaration that we cannot save ourselves. We are powerless in our sin. We are all guilty. In these verses the words "no one" or "none" occur over and over again reminding that no one is righteous, understanding, good, or seeking God. The word "all" is also used repetitively to remind us that we are all guilty sinners undeserving of mercy. The weight of these verses is heavy and hard. And I don't want to spoil it too much, but tomorrow when we begin the next section of the book of Romans, our passage will start with the word "but." This is bad news, but it is this bad news that is the foundation of the good news.

In verses 10 and 11, Paul shows us that our depravity reaches to every part of our being. The doctrine of total depravity is not that we are as sinful as we could possibly be, but instead that every part of us has been tainted by sin. Paul lists out a few of those areas here for us. He begins by telling us that there is none righteous. Apart from God, we have no righteousness of our own. This righteousness speaks of our actions. The things that we do are sinful. And even the things that we do that appear to be good are often rooted in motives that are wrong. This should call our minds back to the theme verses of the book of Romans that told us that those that have received God's righteousness by faith will live. We have no righteousness of our own, but He has made a way.

We are then told that no one understands. This speaks to our thoughts and our minds. Even the way we think has been corrupted by our fallen natures. To the unbeliever the message of the gospel is foolishness (1 Corinthians 2:14). To the world the cross is folly and even offensive, but to believers the cross is everything. It is the power of God (1 Corinthians 1:18, 25). The cross is the message of the gospel, and though the world does not understand it, we know that it is hope for the hopeless and rest for the weary.

The last part of verse 11 tells us that no one seeks after God. This speaks to our desires, and Paul makes it clear that we do not on our own seek after

God. Certainly, there are those that go to church and appear to be religious, but on our own we do not seek Him. We do not yearn for Him or desire Him apart from His Spirit in us. But there is hope. When we were running from Him, the pursuing and initiating love of God has sought after us. Luke 19:10 tells us that Jesus came to seek and save the lost. The beauty of the gospel is that we didn't go looking for it—Jesus came looking for us.

The passage goes on and quotes a plethora of Old Testament Scripture. And every verse is pointing us toward our great need. Paul strategically speaks of different parts of our bodies such as our lips, our feet, our eyes. He is showing again that our depravity has infected us like a cancer. It has spread to every part of us, and the results are devastating. The words of our mouth are for many of us an area of struggle, but the worst thing about sin with our words is that they go much deeper than just the things that we say. Our words reveal what is in our hearts, and when our words are wrong, they are revealing sin in our hearts (Luke 6:45). Our feet are symbolic of our actions, and Paul lists here for us sin that is committed against other people. Sin against other people is a natural outpouring of the condition of our hearts. When our hearts are out of sync with the Spirit, our relationships will be broken. The eyes speak of our pride and lack of humility. Even our faces reveal the sin that is in our hearts. We are desperate for something outside of ourselves.

Who is righteous? No not one. Who is pure? No not one. Who seeks God? No not one.

But there is One. His name is Jesus. He is the Righteous One who covers His people in His own righteousness. He is the One who is pure in deed and thought. He is the One who seeks us. He is the One that finds us. He is the One that pursues us. The weight of our sin is great. It is too heavy for us to bear. Apart from Him we have no hope, but in Jesus there is hope, and every believer is hidden in Him (Colossians 3:3). Our need united us to Him in death, and the power of the gospel has united us to Him in life everlasting. Our hopeless condition is overcome by the God of hope. The gospel is good news.

1. Why is the gospel necessary? Paraphrase this section of Scripture below.

2. Look up the following verses and then record how they relate to this passage in Romans: *Psalm 5:9, Psalm 10:7, Psalm 14:1-3, Psalm 36:1, Psalm 53:1-3, Psalm 140:3, Ecclesiastes 7:20, Isaiah 59:7*

3. These verses point out our weakness and sin. First Paul spoke of our actions, mind, and desires. Which one of these do you struggle with most? How do you find hope in the gospel?

4. Then Paul speaks about our words, actions, and pride. Which one of these is a current struggle? How can you make specific application in one of these areas?

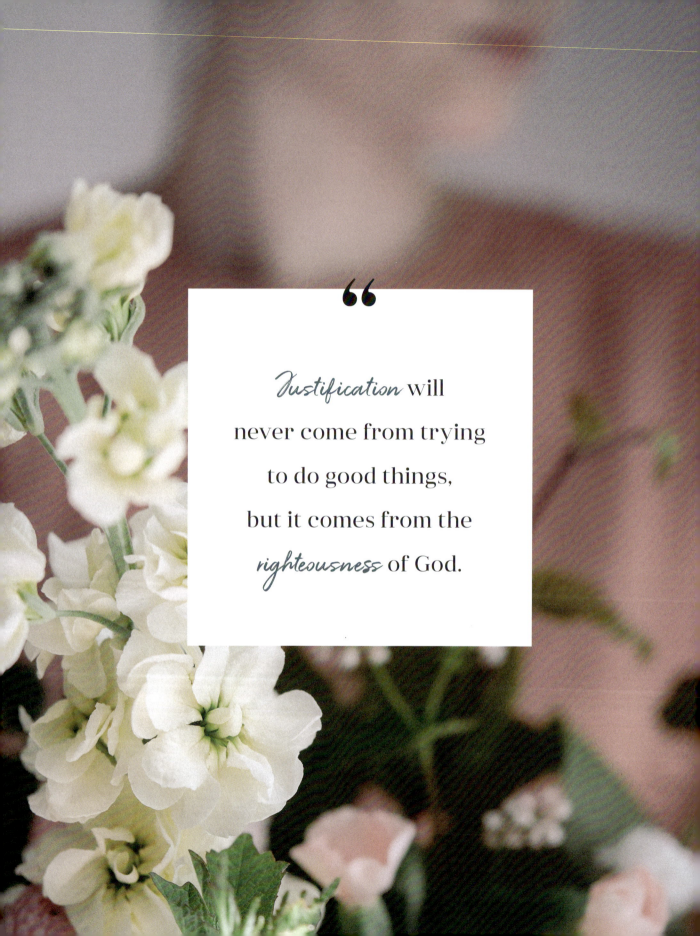

> *Justification* will never come from trying to do good things, but it comes from the *righteousness* of God.

WEEK 3 - DAY 5

HOPE HAS COME

Read Romans 3:21-23

Hope has come, and the gospel changes everything. Up until this point, Paul has been showing us our great need, and now he tells us of our glorious hope. Verse 20 ended with the sobering declaration that the law has no power to save, and we could never be justified through it. Despite that sobering news, there is hope. There is hope in the gospel. There is hope in Jesus. There is justification apart from the law. The tone of Romans has shifted here, and it points to the transforming power of the gospel. The gospel changed everything, and it changes us.

But now. This is how our passage begins. The word "but" is always one that we should pay attention to in Scripture. This common and tiny word so often reveals rich truth to us. That is certainly true here. Though Romans 3:20 ended with the haunting truth that there is no justification through the works of the law, verse 21 overflows with hope. Justification will never come from trying to do good things, but it comes from the righteousness of God. And that righteousness from God is manifested through the person and work of Jesus. The cross brings hope. We must be certain to recognize that this righteousness is not our own. It is a righteousness apart from ourselves. It is a righteousness provided by God.

Though the law has no power to save, the law and the prophets point toward this great salvation. The Old Testament draws our hearts to Jesus. It makes us long with hopeful expectation for the only one that can bring salvation. From the first chapters of Genesis we are left devastated by sin and longing for a Savior. The entire Old Testament gives glimpses and promises about this One that will come to rescue and redeem His people. We must never fall into the trap of thinking that we only need the New Testament. The gospel of the Old Testament is the same as the gospel of the New Testament. Both point to Jesus. Both point to the Cross. Every verse of Scripture declares the story of redemption. The law shows us our sin, but it also points to our Savior (Galatians 3:24). Every word of the Bible points to the hope of redemption.

This righteousness of God is also a righteousness from God, and it is available through faith to all who believe. In salvation we are not only forgiven of our sins, but also clothed in the righteousness of God. This is the great exchange of our sin for the righteousness of Christ (2 Corinthians 5:21). The wording is essential here in helping us understand the mysteries of salvation. It is not our faith that saves us, but the One that we place our faith in. So, we are not saved by faith, but through it. Faith is

merely an instrument. Jesus is the One that saves. Our world talks much about faith. They speak of things like, "just have faith." But this faith is foreign to the faith that the Bible speaks of. The faith present for salvation is not an abstract concept or wishful thinking. This faith is an instrument, and it is in a specific person. Our faith rests in Jesus alone. We place our faith in Him and in His overflowing grace poured out at the cross to cover our sin.

This justification is available through faith to all who will believe, and it is made possible because of Jesus. In these first three chapters, Paul has been making a compelling case for the depravity of man and our great need for redemption. He reminds us again in his presentation of the good news that the bad news of our need is necessary for us to understand the good news of the cross. We cannot divorce our great need from the gospel. We have all sinned. We have all fallen short. We have all missed the mark of God's perfect holiness. We are guilty because of our sin nature inherited from our first father Adam, and we are guilty because of the sins that we have committed. We stand condemned before God and hopeless apart from His grace. But our sorrow turns to rejoicing as we gaze upon the cross and understand what Jesus has done to set us free from the curse of sin.

These words compel us to live a life centered on the gospel. We live rejoicing in the hope that the gospel brings. We praise God the Father for His initiating love in making a way of salvation and pursuing our hearts. We praise Jesus the Son that has lived, died, risen, and ascended for us and united us to Himself. We praise God the Spirit for His transforming and sanctifying power that comforts us in our need and draws us to God. We praise God for His Word that has revealed the message of the gospel to weary hearts. We are brought to worship because of the grace of our God and the joy of salvation.

1 The word "but" marks a pivotal change in the book of Romans. We see a similar thing happen in Ephesians. Read *Ephesians 2:1-10* and record what God has done for us in salvation.

2 Every part of Scripture points to Jesus. Read *Luke 24:13-35* to see how Jesus speaks about the Old Testament. Are there any Old Testament passages that point to Jesus that stand out in your mind?

3 Read *Galatians 3:24* and *Romans 3:20*. What is the purpose of the law?

4 Read *2 Corinthians 5:21*. How does this verse help us to understand the part that the righteousness of God plays in our salvation?

ROMANS 8:7-9

The mind-set of the flesh is hostile to God because it does not submit to God's law. Indeed, it is unable to do so. Those who are in the flesh cannot please God. You, however, are not in the flesh, but in the Spirit, if indeed the Spirit of God lives in you. If anyone does not have the Spirit of Christ, he does not belong to him.

WEEK THREE *Reflection*

READ ROMANS 2:12–3:23

Paraphrase the passage from this week.

What did you observe from this week's text about God and His character?

What does the passage teach about the condition of mankind and about yourself?

How does this passage point to the gospel?

How should you respond to this passage? What is the personal application?

What specific action steps can you take this week to apply the passage?

> There is no room for *boasting* in the life of faith, instead we should *obey* from grateful hearts for the *grace* that we have been given.

WEEK 4 - DAY 1

THE GIFT OF GRACE

Read Romans 3:24-31

These short verses are rich with theological truth that draws our hearts to worship. These verses may be familiar to us, but we can never get over the life-changing gospel truth that is encapsulated in these words. Volumes could be written about each word, and we would still not scratch the surface of the depth of truth contained here.

In verse 24, Paul begins with the glorious pronouncement of justification through grace and redemption through Jesus. Paul speaks of the truth of salvation from every angle in these verses as he seeks to help us grasp the fullness of salvation. The word "justification" has already occurred in the book of Romans, and we have even stated that justification by faith is one of the themes of the book of Romans. Justification is a rich concept that is central to the gospel message. Justification is more than just forgiveness. The doctrine of justification tells us that those that have believed have been declared righteous by God (2 Corinthians 5:21). The children of God stand justified before God of no merit of their own.

This justification is a gift. Salvation is a gift of grace (Ephesians 2:8-9). God's initiating love pursues and redeems those that have defied Him and rebelled against Him. The God we have sinned against is the one that pursues us. The God that in our sin we ran away from has run to us. This is the message of the gospel of grace. God has not only not given us what we do deserve (mercy) but has given us what we do not deserve (grace). God's grace pours out on those that deserve condemnation and He not only forgives our sins, but He also unites us with Christ and declares us to be righteous in Him. In this union with Christ we are in Him and He is in us. And all of this is made possible because of the gospel of grace.

Justification, grace, and redemption are only made possible because of the person of Jesus. There is no salvation apart from Jesus. Paul uses vivid language to communicate deep truths, and the word "redemption" is no different. This word would have brought to mind for those that first read this letter what happened when a slave was purchased or redeemed out of the slave trade. Their ownership was transferred. The word was also a reminder of how God had redeemed His people from Egypt. He delivered them from the bondage of Egypt. In the same way, we who were once slaves to sin have been redeemed from slavery to union with Christ by the price of His own blood (1 Peter 1:18-19). The redemption of our souls is made possible only because of Jesus' work on the cross.

Jesus has done what we could not do for ourselves. Our atonement is substitutionary. Jesus has paid

the price in our place. The debt that we owed was in no way canceled, instead it was taken on Jesus. He is our propitiation or our atoning sacrifice. The word that is used here is the Greek *hilisterion*. The same word is used in the Greek Old Testament (The Septuagint) as the translation for the mercy seat. It is a clear picture of how the Old Testament was pointing forward to Jesus who would be the once for all sacrifice and the One that covers our sin and satisfies the wrath of God in our place. Beginning in Romans 1:18, Paul began to tell of the wrath of God that was revealed, and the good news of the gospel that begins in Romans 3:21 is that there is One that has taken the wrath of God for us. All of God's wrath has been poured out on Jesus. God has put forth Christ as the answer to our sin according to His definite plan (Acts 2:23). The plan has always been the cross, and salvation has always come through Jesus.

God's righteousness is revealed in Jesus and at the cross. Because it is at the cross that we can see that God is both just and our Justifier. He is just because through the cross sin is punished, and He is our justifier because it is through the cross that mercy is shown to the people of God. There is no room for boasting in the life of faith, instead we should obey from grateful hearts for the grace that we have been given. We need a righteous status and we cannot gain it on our own, but in grace it has been provided for us in Jesus. We are saved through faith, but that faith has no power apart from the object of our faith which is Jesus. We have hope because of Jesus. We receive grace because of Jesus. We are justified because of Jesus. We are redeemed because of Jesus. And we have Jesus because God in His initiating love has pursued us.

1   *Paraphrase* these verses below.

2   In what way is *justification* more than forgiveness?

3   Read *1 Peter 1:18-19*. What have we been redeemed with?

4   These verses contain so much powerful truth about what God has done for His children. Take a moment to thank God for all that He has done for you. Write a *prayer of praise* below.

For what does the Scripture say? *Abraham believed God, and it was credited to him for righteousness.*

ROMANS 4:3

WEEK 4 - DAY 2

BY FAITH ALONE

Read Romans 4:1-3

As we enter into this new chapter, we are presented with the timeless truth of salvation by faith in God's grace. Throughout the book of Romans to this point, Paul has been making a point to show us that salvation has always been by grace and that the gospel was revealed in the Old Testament as well (Romans 1:2, 3:21, 31). He has been telling us this, but now he is going to show us. He will use the example of Abraham to show us the message of salvation by grace through faith.

The example that is set forth is Abraham. Abraham was the father of the Jewish people, so he is a fitting example for us in understanding the way of salvation in the Old Testament. Paul sets out to show us that the way of salvation has never changed. It is helpful as we consider Abraham to remember back and refresh ourselves with his story that is found in the book of Genesis. In Genesis 12, God called Abraham to leave his country and his family and everything that he knew to follow the Lord. When this happened, Abraham was not a man of noble or valiant faith, and yet God in His grace set His love on Abraham and called him to Himself. The beginning of Genesis 12 details for us not only the call of Abraham (then Abram), but also the covenant that God made with him to give him a land, a people, and to bless the world through him. God showed him the promised land (Genesis 13:14), and the Lord continued to confirm the covenant promises that He had made to Abraham to give him descendants like the stars in the sky (Genesis 15:5). A pivotal statement about Abraham is made in Genesis 15:6. It is there that we learn that Abraham was justified by faith. Abraham's life continues, and we see the enactment of circumcision (Genesis 17), and the birth of Isaac, the promised son (Genesis 21). In Genesis 22 we see Abraham's willingness to sacrifice Isaac and God miraculously provide a ram to be sacrificed. Abraham's life is marked by the covenant faithfulness of God.

Though Abraham's story took place in the Old Testament before the coming of Jesus, Galatians 3:7-9 tells us that the gospel was preached to Abraham. The gospel has never changed, and the way of salvation has always been by grace through the instrument of faith. Though Abraham was a man respected and revered, he was still a sinful human who was totally incapable of saving himself. Paul uses him as an example to show us and the original readers that if even Abraham had no power to save himself through works, we certainly cannot save ourselves.

We are told that Abraham believed God and that was counted to him as righteousness. Believed God does not mean that he believed in God. It means

that he believed that God would do what He had promised. He believed that a Messiah would come, and it would happen through his line. He was given a veiled glimpse of how God would do it in Genesis 22 when he was asked to sacrifice his son. He was shown that a loving Father would sacrifice his Son on a mountain. He was shown that the gospel is not about what we do for God, but about what God has done for us. Abraham placed his faith in the grace of God and the coming Messiah. He trusted God's Word and His promises. John 8:56 tells us that Abraham rejoiced that he would see the day of Jesus and the he did in fact see it. Though Abraham did not live to see the birth of Jesus, he saw with eyes of faith that God was faithful to His promises. He saw the fulfillment of God's promises in the miraculous birth of his son Isaac, and He knew that God would be faithful to every word of His promises.

Abraham's faith was counted to him or imputed to him as righteousness. This is the great exchange that we have been discussing where believers exchange their sin for the righteous status that only God can give. In this divine transaction, sin is transferred from our account to Christ's, and the righteousness of Christ is applied to our debt. We were hopeless apart from Christ, but God has made a way of salvation. And this way is nothing new. It was set in place before the foundations of the world, and it was set before the believers that have come before us. And God in His grace, mercy, and covenant love has invited us into this grand narrative.

> The gospel has *never changed*, and the way of salvation has always been by *grace* through the instrument of faith.

1. In these verses, Paul points us back to Abraham to show us that people were saved in the Old Testament in the same way that people are today. Paul has brought this up several times. Read *Romans 1:2, 3:21, 31.* Why do you think that Paul wants us to know that this has been God's plan since before the foundation of the world?

2. Why do you think that Paul would have used Abraham as an example of the fact that we cannot be saved by *works*?

3. Sometimes we think that the gospel is about what we do for God when it is actually about what *God has done for us.* How does the life of Abraham remind us of that?

4. How does Abraham's life compel us to *trust God*?

> Salvation is fully a *gift* and *work* of God.

WEEK 4 - DAY 3

A RIGHTEOUSNESS OUTSIDE OURSELVES

Read Romans 4:4-12

Our justification is not of our own doing. Salvation is fully a gift and work of God. Paul continues in this passage to speak of Abraham as well as David to show us that salvation is something that God does. His words bring clarity and stir our hearts to worship at the realization of all that God has done for us.

In verse four, Paul reminds us that salvation is a gift. If there was something that we could do to earn our salvation, it would not be a gift — it would be wages. We do not overflow with gratitude for the kindness of our bosses in paying us what we earned through hard work. Paul is showing us that the same principle is true in salvation. A paycheck is not a gift, but salvation is a gift and that means that there is nothing that we can do to earn it.

Paul turns his attention for a moment to David. David was the greatest of the Israelite kings, and yet he was also a man that succumbed to great sin. Paul quotes David's words from Psalm 32:1-2 as David recognizes that though he had sinned greatly, God did not count his sin against him. The life of blessing is one in which a believer walks in humble assurance that their debt has been paid of no merit of their own. David had made a mess of his life. He had hurt those around him. He had sinned against the Lord. Yet his salvation was not dependent on his supposed goodness, but on God. The truth that there is nothing that we can do to earn salvation brings freedom to our weary hearts. It compels us to live righteously not as a way to earn favor with God, but from a heart left in awe of His love, mercy, and grace.

In God's mercy, He has not given us what we deserved. In His grace, He has given us what we could never have earned on our own. The beauty of the gospel is that God does not simply stop with forgiveness. Through the blood of Christ, we find forgiveness for the sin that separated us from God. And yet, not only have we been forgiven, we have also been clothed in the righteousness of God. God does not simply cancel our debt, He overflows our accounts. So now when God looks at us as His children, He does not see our sin, but instead sees the righteousness of Jesus that has been applied to our lives. The righteousness of Jesus has been imputed to us. This is the doctrine of imputed righteousness. 2 Corinthians 5:19-21 beautifully describe for us how God has not only not counted our sin against us, but also bestowed on us the righteousness of Jesus. Our sin is no longer counted against us, and we are cov-

ered in His righteousness. This is a righteousness that we could never earn, but that has been given to us by a loving Father.

At the end of the passage, Paul turns his attention again to Abraham. He wants to make sure that we are clear about how Abraham was justified. He begins in verse 9 and 10 by asking the question of when Abraham was justified. Was it before his circumcision or after? He is asking whether Abraham was justified by circumcision or by faith. He really wants to drive this point home to us, so he shows us here that Abraham's faith being counted as righteousness happened decades before he was ever circumcised. It is a reminder again that there is nothing that we can do to earn the grace of God. It is a gift. So, Abraham is the father not just of believing Jews that have been circumcised, but also of believing Gentiles that have not been circumcised. His life stands as an example for us that we are justified by nothing that we can do, but freely by God's grace.

This is good news for us. There is nothing that we could do to earn salvation. We cannot fix ourselves. We cannot solve this problem. For many of us this goes against how we like to do it ourselves. But the gospel tells us that we simply can't do it on our own. But the good news is that there is one who not only pays our price, but then covers us in His righteousness. We could live spinning our wheels trying to earn salvation, but Jesus has already earned it for us. Salvation is fully a gift of God. So, we can take a deep sigh of relief and rest in what He has already done for us. He has pursued us. He has paid our debt. He has united us to Christ and clothed us in the righteousness of Jesus. We can simply rejoice with grateful hearts.

The *beauty* of the gospel is that God does not simply stop with forgiveness.

1. Why do you think Paul wanted us to understand that Abraham was justified *before* he was circumcised?

2. Some people at this time trusted in circumcision for salvation. What are some things *today* that people similarly put their trust in?

3. Why is it *comforting* to understand that salvation is a work of God and not something that we can earn?

4. How should understanding what Jesus has done for us *change* the way that we live?

This is why the promise is *by faith*, so that it may be according to grace, to guarantee it to all the descendants — not only to those who are of the law but also to those who are of Abraham's faith. He is the father of us all.

ROMANS 4:16

WEEK 4 - DAY 4

RESTING ON GRACE

Read Romans 4:13-17

Our salvation rests on His grace, and His grace is a solid rock. In the rest of Chapter 4, Paul will continue to look at the life of Abraham as our example of salvation through faith. These verses start with the reminder that the promises made to Abraham did not come through the law; in fact the promises that were made to Abraham were made generations before the law was ever written. Instead, Abraham was justified to God by faith. The law has no power to save. The law reveals our sin to us, and Paul makes the point that knowledge of the law reveals even more how guilty we are. The law of God is good and beautiful, but it cannot redeem. Redemption requires a Redeemer.

The promises of God to Abraham were unconditional promises. They were not dependent on Abraham earning God's favor or being good enough to deserve them. Instead the promises that God made to Abraham in the early chapters of Genesis were completely and totally dependent on God. Our hope rests in His grace alone. There is no better place for us to place our hope because God is firm and secure, and He will do what He has promised that He will do. Grace is God's unmerited favor toward us. It reminds us that not only does God not give us the punishment that we deserve, but He also showers us in His overflowing love and grace. He gives us favor when we deserve punishment. Abraham's justification was not about doing—it was about believing.

Paul then reminds us that everyone that believes is a child of Abraham. Paul stated this at the beginning of chapter 4 (Romans 4:11), and now he speaks again of Abraham as the father of those who believe and the father of the nations. All the way back in Genesis 15:5 God had promised to give Abraham descendants like the stars of the sky. It was a grand promise, but it was also one that seemed impossible. At the time that it was given, Abraham was an old man and he had no children. But the promises of God are not dependent on us. God would keep that promise to Abraham, and you and I as the people of God are evidences of that promise kept. The children of Abraham are not simply those of his physical descent, but instead the offspring of Abraham are all that are Christ's (Galatians 3:29). We are a spiritual Israel. We are descended from Abraham in the faith and share in the blessings of God for His people. The promise made to Abraham on that starry night seemed impossible, but at that very moment as Abraham gazed at the stars, God knew the names of every one of His children that would find their place in Abraham's family through the person of Jesus Christ the Messiah.

Abraham was justified before God because he simply believed that God would do what He had promised. He believed that the impossible was possible with God. Our God is powerful and mighty. He is greater than our obstacles and stronger than our suffering. In salvation, we believe in the finished work of Jesus at the cross and rest in His grace. We are united to Christ and born again to a new life. And every day we must continue to preach the gospel to ourselves and rest in His power. Paul beautifully describes God at the end of verse 17 with an emphasis on His power. He speaks of God as the one that gives life to the dead and speaks into existence things that did not exist. Paul is speaking of God's resurrection power and His creative power. And just as God raised Jesus from the dead and seated Him in glory, in Christ we have been resurrected and seated with Christ (Ephesians 2:5-6). And just as God spoke the world into existence in Genesis 1:1 in the creation by speaking light into darkness, God has spoken the light of the gospel into our hearts to eradicate the darkness (2 Corinthians 4:6). The power of God in the most miraculous of moments is also present in the daily life of the believer. It is that power that sustains us through every moment of our lives.

The gospel is our solid rock and our sure foundation. We rest our faith in His unchanging grace. And just as God kept His promises to Abraham, He will keep His promises to you. The one with the power to set the stars in their place will surely be faithful to every word of His promise.

> The power of God in the most *miraculous of moments* is also present in the *daily life* of the believer.

1. Why does the *law* have no power to save?

2. *Grace is God's unmerited favor.* It is that God not only doesn't give us what we do deserve, He also gives us what we could never earn. How is this evidenced in salvation?

3. Read *Genesis 15:1-6.* Notice how Abraham did not fully understand the promise of God but trusted anyway. Are there any areas of your own life that you don't understand? How can you trust God anyway?

4. How do *God's resurrection and creative power* remind you that you can trust Him in every area of your life?

> Our circumstances *cannot deter* His plans. If God has promised it, it is *as good as done.*

WEEK 4 - DAY 5

HOPE AGAINST HOPE

Read Romans 4:18-25

As we finish Romans 4, Paul speaks one more time of the faith of Abraham. He sets Abraham before us as an example of what it means to be justified by faith. In these final verses of the chapter we are encouraged by the faith of Abraham and encouraged in our own faith as well.

We are told that in hope Abraham believed against hope in the promises of God. Biblical hope is not wishful thinking, but confident expectation. And Abraham believed with that expectant hope that God would do what seemed hopeless and impossible. Abraham recognized that God was his only hope, and the same is true for us as well. God had made a promise to Abraham, and against all the odds, God would keep His promises.

His faith did not weaken, but instead it was strengthened. I love how the text here tells us that Abraham's body was as good as dead. Perhaps it seems like a bit of an exaggeration, but at about 100 years old Abraham and Sarah had no natural chance of having a child. The time had passed, and with each passing day it likely seemed that hope had died with their natural ability to have children. These words present the hopeless condition of Abraham and Sarah of ever having a child, let alone descendants like the stars of the sky. Yet when it says that Abraham's faith did not weaken, it doesn't mean that Abraham never had moments of doubting, but that those moments of doubting did not define his faith. And in fact, those moments of questioning how this was all going to work out were likely the very thing that made him reevaluate his situation and preach to his own heart that God would be faithful despite the impossible situation that was before him. Abraham faced the facts, and then he trusted God anyway. Abraham's faith was not some mystical or personal feeling. Abraham placed his faith in the faithfulness of God.

Though the situation seemed impossible, Abraham trusted that God would keep His promises. Our faith does not depend on our own ability or the strength of our own faith. Our faith rests on the character and promises of God. Abraham clung to the promises of God, and we cling to those promises found in the Word of God. This is why we must make Bible study a priority. As we study God's Word and see His promises to His people, our faith is strengthened, and our hearts are filled with confident, expectant hope. Then like Abraham we can stand fully convinced that God will do what He has said that He will do. The obstacles and impossibilities cannot make our faith waiver when we know that God has promised something. Our circumstances cannot deter His plans. If God has promised it, it is as good as done.

Abraham was not saved by any good works of his own doing. He was not justified by his own goodness, because even Abraham was not good. Instead we are told again that it was his faith that was counted to him as righteousness. And then Paul makes the statement that those words were not recorded for Abraham alone, but also for us. Every word of Scripture in the Old and New Testaments is recorded to point us to the Lord. The way of salvation has never changed, and the words spoken to Abraham instruct our hearts as well. Abraham looked forward to the promise of the Messiah to come.

He trusted that it would be his seed that would one day come to rescue and redeem the people of God. Now you and I as the spiritual children of Abraham look back to Jesus, the promised Messiah that came to redeem us. We look to the one who was delivered up for our trespasses, not simply by men, but by God Himself who had purposed and planned our redemption from before the foundations of the earth (Romans 8:32). He was delivered up so that we could be delivered. He was raised so that we could be justified. Our salvation is the work of His hands and a gift of His grace.

He believed, *hoping against hope*,
so that he became the father of many
nations according to what had been spoken:
So will your descendants be.

ROMANS 4:18

1. What enabled Abraham to *trust God?* What was he trusting God to do?

2. Read *Genesis 18:14* and *Luke 1:37.* How do these words bring comfort for your own life?

3. How does *Bible study* help us to trust God?

4. What is something that you need to *trust God for* in your own life? List out a few character traits of God that can encourage you to trust Him for your specific situation.

ROMANS 8:10-11

Now if Christ is in you, the body is dead because of sin, but the Spirit gives life because of righteousness. And if the Spirit of him who raised Jesus from the dead lives in you, then he who raised Christ from the dead will also bring your mortal bodies to life through his Spirit who lives in you.

WEEK 4 MEMORY VERSE

WEEK FOUR Reflection

READ ROMANS 3:24–4:25

Paraphrase the passage from this week.

What did you observe from this week's text about God and His character?

What does the passage teach about the condition of mankind and about yourself?

How does this passage point to the gospel?

How should you respond to this passage? What is the personal application?

What specific action steps can you take this week to apply the passage?

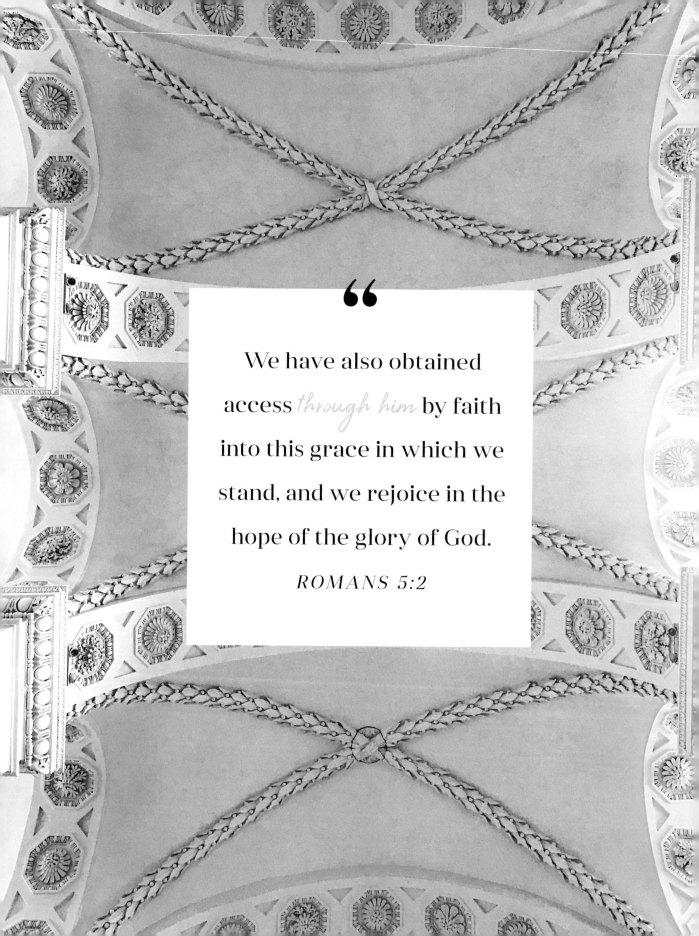

> We have also obtained access *through him* by faith into this grace in which we stand, and we rejoice in the hope of the glory of God.
>
> ROMANS 5:2

WEEK 5 - DAY 1

THE GLORY OF SALVATION

Read Romans 5:1-2

The blessings and benefits of salvation are too numerous to mention at one time, but the beginning of chapter 5 overflows with gratitude for the goodness of the gospel and the great endowment of being united with Christ. The first phrase of the chapter provides us a summary of all that we have studied in Romans so far as it reminds us that we have been justified by faith alone. Because of that justification the spiritual blessings found only in Jesus are poured out on the children of God (Ephesians 1:3). The greatest gift of salvation is the Giver Himself, and every other gift flows from Him. In these verses Paul shifts to the first-person plural and the chapter abounds with pronouns like we, us, and ours. The focus here is on the collective people of God that have been united with Jesus both individually and corporately.

Peace with God comes through our union with Christ because of our justification by faith. Our world is seeking for peace and searching for something that will bring lasting rest. But peace is not a feeling—peace is a person. We have peace with God because of the person of Jesus who is the Prince of Peace. This peace is not just a euphoric feeling; it is a status before God. And as we have learned in our study of Romans thus far, this righteous status is not our own—it is Christ's. Peace is granted to us only because we have been united with the One who is the giver of peace. We have been joined to the one that has borne the wrath of God in our place, and we have been clothed in His righteous status. "Peace" here is the Greek *Eirene* which is the New Testament equivalent to the Hebrew *Shalom*. This does not speak merely of our emotions, but of our wholeness and salvation. Our salvation goes past simple forgivingness and also brings restoration. And all of this is possible only through Jesus Christ.

Verse 2 again begins with "Through Him." All blessing flows through Him. Here we see that it is through Him that not only do we have peace, but also that we have received access. The Old Testament tabernacle and temple pointed us to the presence of God and God's desire to dwell with His people. Yet a peek inside would reveal a curtain that was several inches thick, and this curtain physically and symbolically showed that because of sin mankind was separated from God. In one of the most striking moments of the New Testament we learn that at the moment of Jesus' death that curtain is torn from top to bottom (Matthew 27:50-51). It signaled the breaking of the barrier that stood between God and man. The chasm was closed because the atoning death of Christ had

provided a way of justification. The grace of God displayed at the cross opened the gates of heaven to those that would receive that grace through faith.

We have received this access by faith and into grace. The grace of God is not for the moment of salvation alone—it is the bedrock of our faith. We stand on this grace. Grace has welcomed us into God's presence and called us to live there. We are saved by grace. We stand on grace. We walk in grace.

And we rejoice. We rejoice in confident expectation of the sovereign plan of God unfolding. Our hope rests secure in the glory of God. In Jesus we see the glory of God now (John 1:14, Colossians 1:15-20, Hebrews 1:3), but there is coming a day when we will see fully the glory of our glorious God. In that day, God will fully dwell with His people, and there will be no need for a temple because God will dwell with us (Revelation 21:3, 22). We will experience Emmanuel—God with us like we never have before. "It is all going to be ok" or "the best is yet to come" may seem like trite sayings, but for the people of God these are gloriously true. We place our hope in the One who is our hope knowing that He will do what is good. Our hope rests in the unchanging glory of God, and there is no more secure place for us to place our confidence.

Past, present, and future. Our status of peace with God was declared at the moment of our justification. We have access and walk in His grace in the present, and we rest our hope in a future glory. The glories of salvation are made possible because of Jesus, and we partake in them through our union with Him. The glory of salvation is the Glorious One.

> Grace has *welcomed* us into God's presence and called us to *live there*.

1. Paraphrase *Romans 5:1-2*.

2. Look back at *Romans 5:1-2* and take notice of the word "have." Why do you think this word is significant?

3. These verses show us clearly that these things are made possible through Him. Read *Ephesians 1* and notice the repetition of very similar phrases. Why do you think it is essential that we understand that these things are only possible through Jesus?

4. How does our hope in the *glory of God* change our outlook on our daily life? What circumstance do you need to view through this lens?

And not only that, but we also *rejoice in our afflictions*, because we know that affliction produces endurance, endurance produces proven character, and proven character produces hope.

ROMANS 5:3-4

WEEK 5 - DAY 2

WE REJOICE IN SUFFERING

Read Romans 5:3-5

In the first two verses of chapter five the blessings of salvation roll from the pen of Paul like a symphony that builds with each stanza grander than the last. And then with the first words of verse 3 we can tell that Paul is getting ready for the grand finale. He tells us that despite the riches he has explained to us, it gets even better than that. The blessings of justification are not only peace, access to God, hope, and grace—but also suffering. How can that be? My heart rejoices in all of these beautiful gifts of grace given to me in Christ, but suffering? How can I rejoice in that?

The wording strikes us. Paul doesn't tell us that we rejoice in spite of our suffering or even that we worship in the midst of our sufferings. He tells us boldly that we rejoice in them. Now this does not mean that we pretend to enjoy the things of this world that bring us pain. Instead it means that we trust God so fully that we rejoice in our suffering because we know that it is part of God's sovereign plan for us and for His glory.

After Paul's shocking statement that we rejoice in our sufferings, he begins to unpack the why. We can face our sufferings and rejoice in them because we know that suffering is doing something in us. Suffering makes us who God intends for us to be. Suffering makes us more like Jesus. Paul begins to show us the chain reaction that happens when the child of God faces suffering. The first thing that he tells us is that suffering produces endurance. Suffering brings about the trait of perseverance in our character. There is no other way for this to be formed in us. Suffering produces spiritual formation in us.

The next thing that Paul says is that the endurance produces character. This is Christlikeness. Godly character is formed as we endure the sufferings of this world and turn to the Lord and are transformed into His image. We become like Christ as we suffer and endure in His name. And when all is said and done, suffering produces hope. This is the same hope in the glory of God that was mentioned in verse 2. We have hope because God is faithful. No matter what happens in this world. No matter what life brings. He is faithful to His people.

We have all had moments when our hearts have uttered "Why Lord?" And it is in these moments that we must preach the truth of the gospel to our wandering hearts. Jesus did not promise us a life of ease, but He did promise to go with us. He did not promise that we would be trouble free; in fact He told us that in this world we would face tribulation but that He has already overcome (John 16:33). Over and over again God's Word speaks of suffering and reminds our burdened hearts that the pain

we are facing is not outside of His sovereign grace. With confident expectation and unwavering faith, we can trust that even the deepest sorrows of our souls will be transformed in His hands. We rejoice because the suffering is growing us into His image. We rejoice because our momentary struggles will culminate in glory (2 Corinthians 4:17-18). We rejoice for the joy of suffering for His name (Acts 5:41). We rejoice because suffering has been granted from His hand (Philippians 1:29). We rejoice because just as we share in His suffering, we will also someday share in His glory (Romans 8:17, 1 Peter 4:13). This is our steadfast hope in a world of suffering. We are His. We are in Him and He is in us. We do not walk the path of suffering alone but in union with Christ who has suffered in our place.

And with new covenant language Paul ends this section with a reminder that God's love has been poured into our hearts through the Spirit (Jeremiah 31:33). His love has invaded our hearts and overwhelmed us in grace. We are His. And because we are His we can rejoice in suffering because we know that Jesus is greater than our suffering.

Jesus did not promise us a life of ease, but *He did promise to go with us.*

1. Why do you think Paul would add *suffering* into a list of all the blessings of salvation?

2. Look up the following verses and record your observations about *suffering* in the life of the believer: *John 16:33, Romans 8:17, 2 Corinthians 4:17-18, James 1:2, 1 Peter 4:12-13*

3. How has *suffering* played a part in your own walk with God?

4. How does this passage give hope in the current situations in your life right now?

> God in His *initiating love* had purposed before the foundation of the earth the plan of redemption.

WEEK 5 - DAY 3

THE INITIATING LOVE OF GOD

Read Romans 5:6-8

God's love is displayed at the cross. His initiating and pursuing love is demonstrated in the wonder that the high and holy God would send His Son to condescend to humanity and then go to the cross. It is interesting to see this passage in the context of the verses that came right before. Paul speaks to believers in the context of suffering. He wants to remind us of the extravagant love of God on our behalf. He compels us to praise as he reminds us that the love of God has been poured into our hearts, and then he pauses to explain just how that has happened.

Paul first states our condition. We were weak. We were destitute and depraved. We were lost in our sin and without hope. But God. In our broken and helpless state Christ came. He came at the right time or the appointed time. God in His initiating love had purposed before the foundation of the earth the plan of redemption (1 Peter 1:20, Acts 2:23). Jesus was always the plan. And then at the appointed time Jesus came to carry out the sovereign plan of God. Jesus came while we were weak. He went to the cross when we were rebellious and ungodly. He chose us when we were incapable of choosing Him.

Paul speaks also of the incompressible love of God. Not only is God's love initiating in seeking after us when we were lost, but it is also beyond our comprehension. The love of God does not make sense to our human minds. Why would God set His love on His people from eternity past? Perhaps this love would make sense if we were good or righteous people, but these first chapters of Romans have given a vivid picture of our condition. We have nothing to offer Him, and yet He has given us everything. He has given us Himself.

God shows His love for us by sending His son. For God so loved the world that He gave (John 3:16). He gave the most precious thing for us though we were filthy and broken and dead in our sins. Jesus went to the cross out of love for us. He was beaten and bruised. He was shamed and reviled. He was bloody and humiliated. The God of the ages hung on the cross for the very people whose sins He bore there. As the crowd pierced through the silence with screams for his crucifixion, He bore our humiliation. As the crown of thorns was pressed into his skin, He carried our shame. As the pain jolted through His body with every smack of the hammer as the nails were driven into His hands and feet, our names were in His mind. As the pain surged through His body and the end drew near, His love for us did not waver. As He uttered the words, "It is finished," He secured our redemption. He did what He had come to do. He paid the price while we were yet sinners.

The weight of the cross and the blackness of that day when the sun went dark points to the Light of the

Word. The heaviness of Calvary reminds of the burden removed from us as our sins are forgiven. The depth of our need proclaims the greatness of the salvation Jesus has purchased with His own blood.

So why should we think about our own desperate need and His glorious redemption in light of our suffering? Because what greater comfort for our darkest days than to be reminded of what God has done for us. What could instill greater hope than seeing how God has transformed the horror of the cross into the most grace-filled moment in all of history. The God that used the suffering of the cross to bring the glory of redemption will transform your suffering and sorrow to glory one day as well. For every moment we would doubt His love, we can look to the cross. For every moment that His plan does not makes sense, we can look to the cross. We fix our gaze to this moment when at the appointed time Jesus bore our sin and cleansed our shame.

His *initiating and pursuing love* is demonstrated in the wonder that the high and holy God would *send His Son* to condescend to humanity and then *go to the cross*.

1. Paraphrase the passage below.

2. What do these verses teach you about the way that *God loves His people*?

3. Jesus was always the plan to redeem us. He was not Plan B. Read *1 Peter 1:20* and *Acts 2:23*. How does this truth bring you comfort?

4. What does this passage teach us about *who God is* and *what He has done* for us?

For if, while we were enemies, we were reconciled to God through the death of his Son, then *how much more*, having been reconciled, will we be saved by his life.

ROMANS 5:10

WEEK 5 - DAY 4

WE REJOICE

Read Romans 5:9-11

Language does not contain enough words to adequately describe our God or the blessings of salvation. Paul finishes this section by reiterating the truth he has already written and trying to convey with words what words could never fully explain. The hymn "The Love of God" comes to mind as its words express how inexpressible God's love is for us. "The love of God is greater far than tongue or pen could ever tell" the song proclaims. It goes on to exclaim that if the ocean was filled with ink and the skies were our parchment, we would empty the oceans and fill the skies of parchment before we could fully explain God's love for His people. As we seek to convey the depth of His love for us, our words fail. His love is greater and deeper and more extravagant than our words can express.

As we come to these verses we again see Paul heralding the wonder of salvation. Our salvation, our assurance, and our joy rest in the finished work of the cross. Paul wants us to see that God's love displayed in salvation instills in our hearts confidence for the future. The love of God displayed through the gospel gives us hope in sorrow and joy for our journey.

We see in these verses the already but not yet of our salvation. Our salvation is in many ways past, present, and future. Our justification happens in an instant, our sanctification happens over a lifetime, and our glorification will happen in the end. So, though we are saved, we are constantly growing in our salvation. And though we are saved, we are awaiting a day when we will see the full benefits of that salvation. We have been justified already and placed in Christ, awaiting the day when sin and sorrow will be no more for the people of God, and we will dwell with God forever.

Throughout these verses, Paul uses several times the reasoning "How much more." Paul is reminding us of the trustworthiness of God. If God has saved us, how much more can we trust Him to keep us. If He has rescued and redeemed us, how much more can we expect Him to carry us through this life. If He has given us His own Son, how much more can we trust Him to give us everything that we need. If He has poured out His wrath on Jesus instead of on us, how much more can we trust that He will pour out His mercy and grace on us for each day. What He has started we know that He will bring to completion (Philippians 1:6). He will do what He has said that He will do.

In verse 11, Paul draws this section to a close. After all that he has just written, he says, "more than that." We rejoice. We rejoice because of the love of God. We rejoice for the hope of salvation. We

rejoice because even in suffering we have hope. We rejoice in our God for who He is and what He has done. True joy comes from understanding the gospel and its implications for our daily lives. This is what is meant when we say that we must preach the gospel to ourselves. When the obstacles of life lay before us, we remind ourselves that God has overcome every obstacle for us through the cross. When suffering threatens to steal our hope, we remember that our hope is not found in the things of this world, but in the God who has already overcome. No matter what may come, we rest in the finished work of the cross. We rest in the truth that though we were desperate and destitute sinners, we are now a new creation in Him. We rejoice because of who He is. We rejoice because of what we once were and what He has transformed us to be. We rejoice that even in sorrow, and suffering, and waiting, He is faithful. We rejoice in Him.

Our *justification* happens in an instant,
our *sanctification* happens over a lifetime,
and our *glorification* will happen in the end.

1. Paraphrase these verses.

2. How does the gospel give us *hope*?

3. How can you practically remind yourself of the *joy* found in the gospel this week?

4. Write out a *prayer thanking God* for all that He has done for you and for who He is.

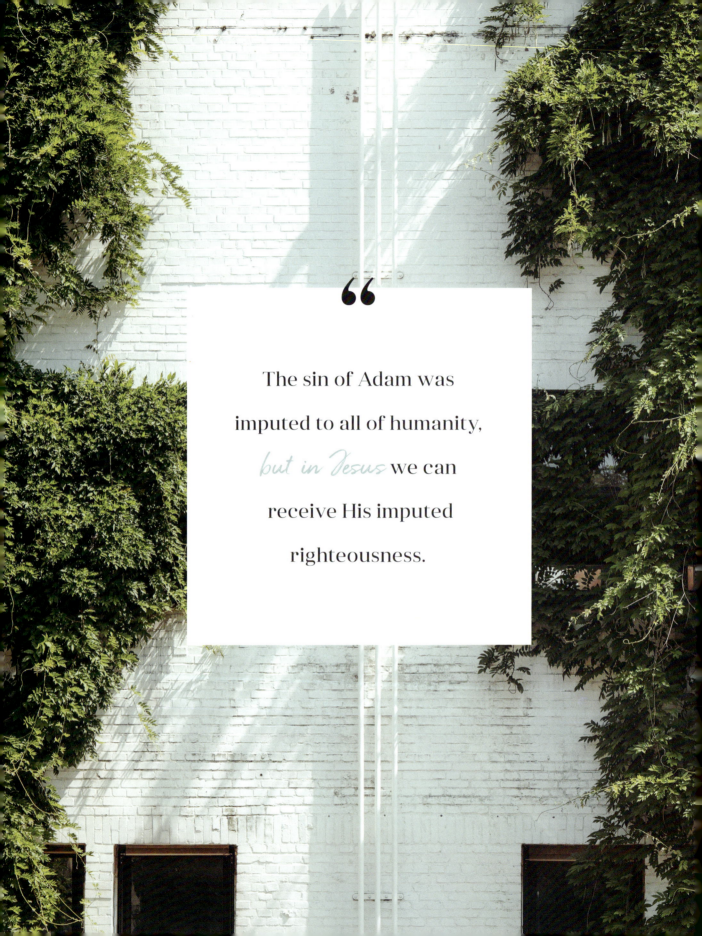

> The sin of Adam was imputed to all of humanity, *but in Jesus* we can receive His imputed righteousness.

WEEK 5 – DAY 5

THROUGH ONE MAN

Read Romans 5:12-14

As we begin to look at the second half of Romans 5 we continue to see the deep theology that Paul wants to explain to us. Paul takes us all the way back to the beginning. In the second half of this chapter he is going to compare Adam and Jesus and show us how they are our representatives. Adam is presented to us as our covenant head, the representative for all of humanity. Paul presents here the doctrine of original sin. We are all born as sinners. We are condemned because we are born sinners, and because of our personal sin. The first chapters of Romans gave us a clear picture of the depravity of humanity apart from Jesus, and here Paul reiterates those truths. Without Jesus, we are hopeless.

After the glorious creation in Genesis 1 and 2 comes the devastation of the fall in Genesis 3. It is here that we see Adam and Eve choose sin over God. It is here that one moment changes all of humanity and all of history. In Genesis 3 the consequences of sin are listed out for us. Sin always brings death. And this sin would bring into the world both physical and spiritual death. But tucked in this key chapter is a promise. It is a promise of a Redeemer. It is a promise of a second Adam.

Adam was the representative for all of humanity, and in Genesis 3 he failed the test. Through him sin and death spread to all of humanity. Before salvation every person is considered to be "in Adam." We are identified with him in his sin and rebellion against God. We are considered guilty. But these verses do more than point us to the terrible news that we are represented by Adam and condemned to death because we are sinners. Verse 14 gives a glimmer of hope that we will be able to examine further as we look at the rest of the chapter.

The glimmer of hope is this. Adam is a type of the one who was to come. Adam was pointing to someone. We will soon see that the One that Adam points to is Jesus. Just as Adam is our representative in sin, so Jesus is the representative of all those who will believe. The sin of Adam was imputed to all of humanity, but in Jesus we can receive His imputed righteousness. Theologians often refer to these verses when describing the covenant of works and the covenant of grace. The covenant of works is the status of mankind before the fall when man was judged on his works. The covenant of grace is what we see instituted in Genesis 3 as God covers Adam and Eve with coats of skins and provides the promise of a Redeemer. After the fall, God made it clear that the only way humanity could be reconciled to Him was through the saving work of the Messiah. In the Old Testament we see believers looking forward to the coming Redeemer. We

saw this in chapter 4 when we looked at the life of Abraham who was justified by faith. Now we are justified as we look back to the Messiah who has already come.

So, Adam was a type of the one to come. He was an example, a foreshadowing, and an illustration of what Jesus would do. Just as we are made sinners through the work of Adam, so we can be made righteous through the work of Christ.

Sin came into the world and it changed everything. Jesus came into the world and changed everything. These verses show us clearly the destitute condition that we are in apart from Jesus, but it also gives us tremendous hope. Our only hope is for our hearts to be transformed by the gospel. Our wicked hearts can be made new. And there will be a day for the people of God when death and sin and sorrow will be no more. We rejoice in that hope.

> **Therefore, just as sin entered the world *through one man*, and death through sin, in this way death spread to all people, because all sinned.**
>
> ROMANS 5:12

1. Paraphrase these verses.

2. Read *Genesis 3*. How did Satan tempt Adam and Eve? How might he tempt us in the same ways?

3. Read *Genesis 3:21* and note how God clothed them. This is the first picture of an atoning sacrifice. Compare the following verses that reference the people of God being clothed: *Isaiah 61:10, Romans 13:14, Galatians 3:27, Ephesians 4:24, Colossians 3:10-17*. What are believers clothed with?

4. How do Adam and all of the Old Testament *point to Jesus*?

ROMANS 8:12-14

So then, brothers and sisters, we are not obligated to the flesh to live according to the flesh, because if you live according to the flesh, you are going to die. But if by the Spirit you put to death the deeds of the body, you will live. For all those led by God's Spirit are God's sons.

WEEK FIVE Reflection

READ ROMANS 5:1-14

Paraphrase the passage from this week.

What did you observe from this week's text about God and His character?

What does the passage teach about the condition of mankind and about yourself?

How does this passage point to the gospel?

How should you respond to this passage? What is the personal application?

What specific action steps can you take this week to apply the passage?

> When sin had us trapped, grace *rushed in* and set us free.

WEEK 6 - DAY 1

GRACE ABOUNDED ALL THE MORE

Read Romans 5:15-21

In verses 12-14 of chapter 5, we saw that in Adam we are all counted as sinners. We are guilty in Adam. At the end of verse 14 we saw the glimmer of hope that Adam was a type of the one to come. Adam was pointing to someone greater. In the first Adam we are all made sinners, but in the Last Adam there is hope for the broken sinner (1 Corinthians 15:45-49). Though through the first Adam sin and death are part of our nature, we can have a new nature through the second Adam (2 Corinthians 5:17). Everything changes because of Jesus.

These verses draw our minds to Ephesians 2 where the case of our sinfulness is stated in much the same way as in the book of Romans. We are reminded that we are utterly helpless without Him. Every aspect of our being has been corrupted by our sin natures. In Ephesians 2:1-3 we see the dire condition of our humanity. We were dead, and a dead person has no power to raise ourselves. We had no hope. We needed resurrection. We needed regeneration. But then come the glorious words of Ephesians 2:4 in the same way as Romans 5:15 declaring a great but. Though we were hopeless and dead in our sin, but God has made us alive. He has united us to Christ. When sin had us trapped, grace rushed in and set us free.

Throughout the passage Paul uses several times wording similar to "much more" as a way of showing that though we were devastated by the sin of Adam, the grace of Jesus is so much greater than the sin of Adam. Our salvation and justification does not simply return us to the state that Adam was in before the fall. It does so much more than that. Before the fall we see Adam in a state of innocence. We do not return to this innocent state where we are just not guilty of sin, instead we are given the positive righteousness of Jesus. We are forgiven, and our debt is paid, but our account is not left at zero, it is filled to overflowing with the righteousness of Jesus.

We are lavished in the gift of grace, and a gift cannot be earned. This gift is freely given to us. Through the Old Testament we see the law, but just as Paul has been reminding us in these first few chapters—the law never had any power to save. The law could not save, but it could point us to our weakness and our need. The law makes us long for a Savior. And Jesus is the only one that can fill that longing in our hearts. Sin has left us broken, but through Christ we are restored. Grace is the antidote for sin.

In Jesus we do not find just enough grace to get by. In Him we find grace upon grace (John 1:16).

We find superlative ever abounding grace that sustains us through this life and draws us to His side. Though in Adam we are made sinners, when we are justified we are in Christ. Our union with Christ changes everything. We are in Him and He is in us. Where sin increased, grace abounded all the more. Grace overflowed to us. This passage is overflowing with kingdom language. In it we see that part of our union with Christ is a transfer of kingdoms. Through Adam we are born into the kingdom of this world. It is a kingdom that is corrupted and always leads to death. Death reigns in the kingdom of this world. But in the kingdom of God, grace reigns. We are transferred from the kingdom of death to the kingdom of grace. From death to abundant life. From the kingdom of this world, to the kingdom of God.

Grace reigns through righteousness, and it leads us to life eternal. And it is all possible because of our union with Christ. Through justification by faith, we are united to Jesus. We are no longer identified as the children of Adam, but as the children of God. And this union with Christ and the grace that has been lavished on us should change the way that we live. Just as grace rushed in and brought us back to life, we must allow that same grace to work sanctification in us. Through His grace and as we abide, we will be transformed more and more into His image.

> We are *lavished* in the gift of grace, and a gift cannot be earned. This gift is *freely given* to us.

1. Read *Ephesians 2:1-10*. How do these verses give you insight to what God does for us through salvation?

2. Throughout the passage Paul uses the phrase "much more" as he *contrasts Adam and Jesus*. Why do you think he does this? In what ways is what we receive from Jesus much greater than what we receive from Adam?

3. His grace abounds. *It is more than enough for us.* What do you learn about the abounding grace of God as you see the depth of our depravity?

Therefore we were buried with him by baptism into death, in order that, just as Christ was raised from the dead by the glory of the Father, so we too may *walk in newness of life.*

ROMANS 6:4

WEEK 6 - DAY 2

IN NEWNESS OF LIFE

Read Romans 6:1-4

Paul eloquently answers his critics and the critics of grace through faith in salvation. Paul has spent so much time on justification by faith, and now he turns to those that would seek to undermine the gospel. If Romans were to be written in our current time it would almost be as though Paul anticipates the negative social media comments and answers them before his critics have a chance to ask them. The first question is one that arises often when the gospel is preached. Does grace fan the flame of sin? If God's grace is so great and abounding, should we keep sinning so that God's grace can shine brighter?

In many ways the first part of Romans addresses those that would tend toward legalism. Legalism is when people try to add works to God's grace in salvation. The legalist wants to earn salvation through good works. But now Paul addresses a different perspective. This view is called the antinomian view. It is an anti-law view that looks at salvation and says that salvation is great because now we can do whatever we want, and God's grace will cover it. Paul's response to whether believers should keep on sinning? By no means! Paul is showing us that what Jesus has done for us fundamentally changes who we are. The gospel doesn't just change what we do, it changes who we are. But before we dismiss this view we must think about how we sometimes live with this spirit even if we would never utter these words. When we think our sin is no big deal, we are having this same attitude. We must examine our own hearts and heed the words of Paul here in the book of Romans.

Paul expounds his initial reaction to this objection by explaining why we must not continue in sin. The first thing that he speaks of is the truth that believers have died to sin, so how could we continue to live in it? In Romans 6:2 the word "died" is in the aorist tense in the Greek. This shows that it is a past event or a done deal. Though there is a sense in which we continue to die to sin, there is also a sense in which this is something that happened for the believer in the past. Salvation has aspects that are past, present, and future. Paul here points to the past event. The moment of our salvation has reckoned us dead to sin. In this life we will still struggle with sin and fight against it, but there will come a day when sin is defeated once and for all. The gospel is strong enough to not only redeem and forgive us from sin, but also to help us to turn from sin each day. God's grace justifies us and will one day glorify us, but right now it is sanctifying us. It is ever increasingly transforming us into the image of God. It is making us who He has made us to be. It is making us holy.

Paul then uses the illustration of baptism. We must be careful to note that Paul is in no way saying that baptism saves us. He has spent chapters building the case for justification by faith alone, and he is not in any way saying that baptism is necessary for salvation. Instead he is telling us that baptism is an outward symbol of an inward reality. Water baptism is a symbol of what happens when a person is justified and united to Christ. It is a picture of our union with Christ. Through the waters of baptism, we picture what has happened to us in salvation. As we are buried into the death of Jesus and raised up from the waters we picture that our old man has died and been buried with Christ, and now we are raised to walk in newness of life. We are resurrected people. We have been made new and regenerated by the work of the Spirit in us. Though we were dead and unable to raise ourselves, we are raised by the power of God. And because of the resurrection of Jesus, we are raised to live a resurrection life. We are raised to a new life. No longer should we live in sin, but instead we should live for Jesus who died for us and is raised for us.

> **The gospel is *strong enough* to not only redeem and forgive us from sin, but also to help us to turn from sin each day.**

1 How can we live with the antinomian attitude that *sin isn't a big deal*? Do you catch yourself struggling more with the side of legalism or the side of not taking sin as seriously as you should?

2 How should the knowledge that *we are dead to sin* change the way that we live?

3 How does *baptism* picture our salvation and union with Christ?

4 Why should the gospel compel us to *live a new life*?

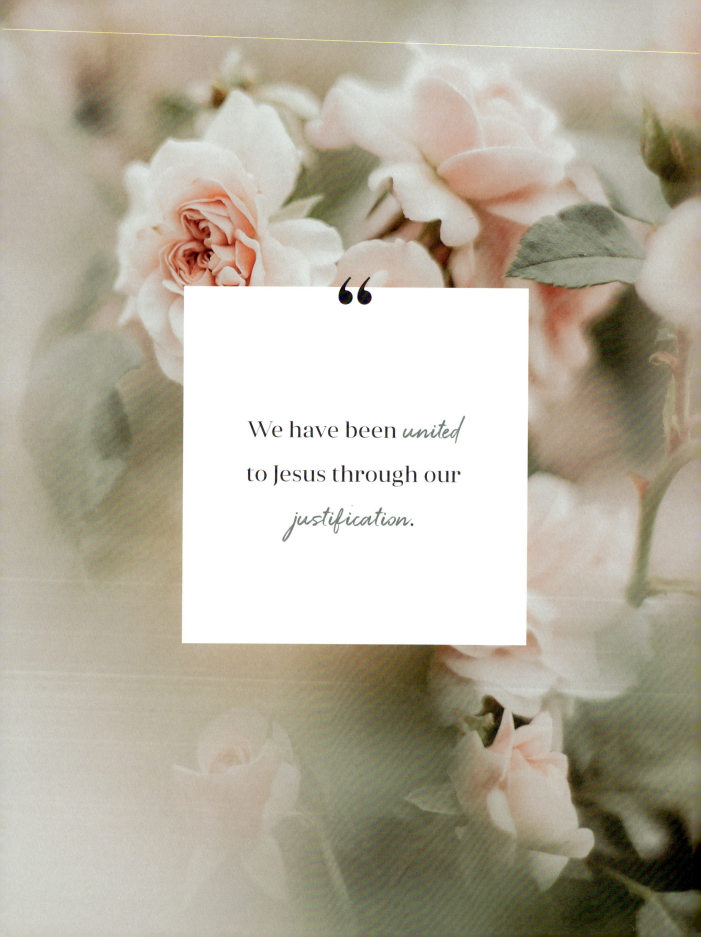

> We have been *united* to Jesus through our *justification*.

WEEK 6 - DAY 3

UNITED TO CHRIST

Read Romans 6:5-14

The opening chapters of Romans focused on our justification, but now we are making a shift to addressing our sanctification. But before Paul speaks about how we should live, He reminds us of who we are. He reminds us of who we are and whose we are. He reminds us that holiness and godliness are made possible because we are united to Jesus Himself. And our union with Christ changes everything.

We have been united to Jesus through our justification. We have died to sin and we have been raised to walk in newness of life. We are no longer what we once were, we are a new creation. In this passage we are not being commanded to muster up some strength of our own or to try harder. We are being commanded to be who we are. We are being commanded to live in light of the reality of our union with Christ. The power of the resurrection propels us forward to live lives of holiness. Salvation and our union with Christ not only compel us to obedience, they also make it possible. Before salvation we were dead in our sin, but now we have died to sin. Without Jesus we had no power to stop sinning, we had no power over our sin nature. But now we are new people. We now have the power through the Spirit to not sin. We no longer have to sin. Now certainly, I am not proposing that we will be perfect after salvation or obtain perfection in this world, but now through the power of Christ in us we can flee from sin.

As believers, we have a new identity. We are in Christ and He is in us. We are no longer under the reign of sin, but instead we are under the reign of grace (Romans 5:21). We have not only died to sin, but we now live to God. He is everything to us, and everything that we do should be for Him and to Him. In life and in death we live for Him and for His glory (Romans 14:8, Acts 17:28, Philippians 1:21). Jesus made a once for all sacrifice that has brought us near to God and allowed us to live free from the overwhelming power of sin.

Justification compels us to sanctification. Justification is fully and wholly a work of God. Sanctification is a work of God as well and yet He invites us in to join Him in this process. He invites us to live like who He has made us to be. He calls us to flee from sin and to submit to the Lord (James 4:7-10). Our sanctification is made possible by the work of the Spirit within us. We cannot do this on our own, but with the power of the Spirit in us we can surrender to God and pursue godliness. The Word of God that is living and active convicts us of sin and spurs us on to holiness (Hebrews 4:12). Through the power of God in us we can be sanctified to be more like Him.

Instead of yielding to sin over and over and over again and being powerless to change, as believers with the Spirit of God inside of us and through our union with our Savior, we can present ourselves to God (Romans 12:1). We have been brought from death to life. We that were once identified with Adam are now identified with Jesus. We were chosen before the foundation of the world to be His own and to grow in holiness for the praise of His glory (Ephesians 1:3-6). Sin no longer must have dominion over us. We are His.

The gospel has the power not only to justify us, but also to sanctify us. We do not have to do this on our own. There will be times when we fail and yield to sin, and yet those are the moments that we can preach the gospel to ourselves and remind our hearts of what Jesus has done for us and of who we are in Him. Little by little we will grow in godliness. Little by little we will be sanctified by Him. Little by little we will grow in grace until the day we see Him face to face.

> For if we have been *united* with him in the likeness of his death, we will certainly also be in the likeness of his resurrection. For we know that our old self was crucified with him so that the body ruled by sin might be rendered powerless so that we may *no longer be enslaved* to sin
>
> ROMANS 6:5-6

1. How should *who we are in Christ* change the way that we live?

2. Why does our *justification* compel us to sanctification?

3. What are some ways that you can *grow in godliness*?

4. How does the gospel give you *hope* for the days that you fail?
   How can we *grow* in the Lord even through repentance of our sin?

Don't you know that if you offer yourselves to someone as obedient slaves, *you are slaves of that one you obey* — either of sin leading to death or of obedience leading to righteousness?

ROMANS 6:16

WEEK 6 - DAY 4

SLAVES TO RIGHTEOUSNESS

Read Romans 6: 15-19

As chapter 6 continues, Paul restates in verse 15 what he had said in verse 1. He is driving home the point, though now with a different illustration, that the grace of God compels us to righteousness and not to lives of sin. When grace is preached, it is expected that some would misunderstand and view it as permission to sin. Yet this perspective shows that their hearts have not been captured by the incomprehensible grace of God. Does grace compel us to sin, by no means Paul declares! In fact, he will tell us that the exact opposite is true. Grace compels us to righteousness.

Paul uses the example of slavery. He uses imagery that denotes us as slaves or servants and then shows us how there are only two masters that can control us. We can either be controlled by our sin and be sinking deeper and deeper in our degradation, or we can be controlled by righteousness and the Righteous One and be growing in sanctification and godliness. We are either unbelievers enslaved by our depravity, or we are believers that have hearts to serve God alone.

Paul tells us that we are slaves to the one that we obey. He tells us that we can be slaves to sin and that the result of that relationship is always death. Our world so often thinks that they can live in sin and still be ok. Some people even think that they can live how they want and attend church on Sunday and somehow everything will be ok. But sin always leads to death. This was promised in the first chapters of Genesis and it has always been true. In one sense there is physical death that is a result of sin entering this world through the fall, but there is also a life of death filled with the consequences of lack of peace that a life of sin brings. But there is good news. There is another option. Instead of being a slave to sin, you can serve a different master. Instead of reaping death, you can find righteousness and life eternal. The gospel confronts us with our weakness and sets before us only two possibilities.

Verse 17 bursts through with thanksgiving at the magnificence of the gospel that Paul has been proclaiming. Thanks be to God for the gospel. Though we were slaves to sin, Jesus became sin for us. Though we were condemned to death, Jesus died in our place. The gospel shows another way. The gospel points to Jesus. The gospel points to the cross where hope is found for the weary sinner enslaved to sin. The gospel is hope for the one enslaved to pride, lust, anger, addiction, and self-righteousness. The gospel is the only hope. By the grace that He freely bestows on us and through His regenerating work we are made into new creations. We are redeemed. A word that literally means that we are bought back. We are bought out of the slave trade

of sin and given a new kind of master and a new kind of freedom. And freedom in Christ isn't the freedom to do whatever we want, it is the freedom to live for Him.

God transforms our hearts and our minds. He transforms our actions and our motives. He changes us not from the outside in, but from the inside out. Sin leads to ever increasing sin. It is a slippery slope that takes us lower and lower. But holiness and righteousness do the opposite. As we grow in righteousness we are growing in sanctification and being transformed into His image. He is the One that does the work. As we come to His Word and behold His radiant character, we are transformed in His presence. Because you cannot see God and not be changed.

We all have a master. In this passage we are called to evaluate ourselves to see who our master is. Are we slaves to our own desires that lead us to sin, or have we been transformed by the grace of God and are now slaves to righteousness? And if we are the people of God, are we living in light of our union with Christ? Are we putting to death the sin that Jesus has already paid for? Are we resting in His work of sanctification in us and cooperating with the Spirit? Are we in His Word so that we will know who He is? Are we growing in sanctification until the day we see His face?

> He changes us *not from* the outside in, *but from* the inside out.

1 Why might some people think that *grace* is permission to sin?

2 How is the gospel the *answer* to the problem of sin?

3 In what ways does sin *lead* to more sin? In what ways does righteousness *lead* to more righteousness?

> *Sin* makes you think that you are free while its *chains* wrap around you tighter and tighter.

WEEK 6 - DAY 5

BE WHO YOU ARE

Read Romans 6:20-23

As chapter 6 comes to a close we see the end of Paul's second answer to the question of whether we should keep on sinning because of God's grace. Paul's answer is by no means, but he also takes time to explain his reasoning. In verses 1-14 of the chapter he reminds us of our union with Christ. Our union with Christ compels us to newness of life. We have been united to Christ and now we live in Him and with Him in us. In verses 15-23, Paul reminds us that we are not our own and that we have a new master. We were once slaves to sin, but now we are slaves to righteousness.

In these verses, Paul speaks of the fruit of righteousness and the fruit of sin. He reminds us that things aren't always as they appear. It may seem like unbelievers are "free," but the so-called freedom that they have always leads to death, because sin leads to death. Some people may look at Christians and say that they are not free and that they are living under rules and regulations, but Paul reminds us that righteousness leads to sanctification which leads to life. The so-called freedom of sin is truly bondage and the constraints of righteousness is what gives us true freedom. Sin makes you think that you are free while its chains wrap around you tighter and tighter. But God is the freedom giver.

The children of God have been set free from sin. This is past tense. We are free from sin's penalty, and as we grow in sanctification we are being freed from its power over us. And some day we will be free from its presence. Sin is the enemy that we have been set free from as the children of God. We must not return again and again to our enemy. So, when sin and temptation come knocking, we can preach to ourselves again and again that we have been set free. We can preach to ourselves that sin no longer has dominion over us. We can preach to ourselves that we have a new master.

Over and over throughout Scripture we see that the indicative comes before the imperative. This is the argument that Paul brings in chapter 6. We must know who we are before we can do what we are supposed to do. God is first concerned with our inward being and then with our outward doing. We are being called to be who we are. We are being called to remember what God has done for us and live like it. We have been set free from sin, so instead of returning and presuming on God's grace we can flee from sin and run to God who is a far greater master.

The fruit of our salvation is our sanctification. This is the process of us ever increasingly being transformed by God into the image of God. Sanctifica-

tion isn't a DIY for us to work on. "Do it yourself" just doesn't work in this process. Instead it is the process of being transformed by God and for God. God asks us to cooperate with Him in this work, but it is still His work. We have no power to make ourselves holy, but as we submit and surrender to Him, He transforms us little by little. As we behold His glory, He transforms us from one degree of glory to another (2 Corinthians 3:18). Little by little He transforms us into who He has already made us to be.

There are two fruits in this passage. The fruit of sin that leads to death and the fruit of righteousness that leads to our sanctification. Thomas Watson wrote, "Till sin be bitter, Christ will not be sweet." The fruit of sin must become so bitter to us that we want no part of it in our lives. And sin becomes bitter as we behold our God and His glory. As we behold Him in His Word and grow in sanctification He changes our desires. A desire for sin and the consequences it brings is replaced with a desire for God and the fruit of sanctification. And little by little He transforms us. The chapter ends with one of the most famous verses in Romans. It sums up the message of the book in just a few words. There are two paths. There are the earned wages of sin where we get what we deserve, or this is the free gift of God's grace. There are only two paths. The path of rejecting God and living for sin and self that ends in death, and the path of surrender to God's sovereign grace that ends in life. The way of the world leaves man empty, but the gospel brings peace and fellowship with God. It gives life with God right now, and life with Him forever more.

> The so-called freedom of sin is *truly bondage* and the constraints of righteousness is what gives us *true freedom.*

1 In what ways is the "freedom" of sin actually *bondage*?

2 *Sanctification* is something that God does. How does this reminder free us from trying to live in our own strength?

3 After studying *Romans 6*, how would you answer the question of if we should keep sinning because of God's grace?

ROMANS 8:15-16

For you did not receive a spirit of slavery to fall back into fear. Instead, you received the Spirit of adoption, by whom we cry out, "Abba, Father!" The Spirit himself testifies together with our spirit that we are God's children

WEEK 6 MEMORY VERSE

WEEK SIX *Reflection*

READ ROMANS 5:15–6:23

Paraphrase the passage from this week.

What did you observe from this week's text about God and His character?

What does the passage teach about the condition of mankind and about yourself?

How does this passage point to the gospel?

How should you respond to this passage? What is the personal application?

What specific action steps can you take this week to apply the passage?

> We have been *united to Him* for a distinct purpose.

WEEK 7 - DAY 1

FREE TO SERVE

Read Romans 7: 1-6

We have died to sin, and chapter 6 pointed us to that glorious reality. Now in chapter 7 Paul will remind us that we have also died to the law. Our union with Christ frees us from bondage to sin and to the law and frees us to service and surrender that is enabled by the Spirit of God in us. While chapter 6 reminded us that we have a new master, chapter 7 will remind us that we have a new relationship.

Paul speaks to his brothers and sisters in the faith. He fervently wants them to understand the implications of the new relationship and new life they have been called to live in. He uses an illustration that is most fitting in the situation. It is an illustration that nearly all will have partaken in through experience or through the experience of someone that they know. He uses earthly marriage as an illustration of our relationship to Jesus. It is fitting because marriage in itself is a picture of the church's relationship with Christ (Ephesians 5). This earthly union points to a spiritual union between Jesus and His bride. Earthly marriage is a living and breathing picture of our relationship to Jesus. It puts the gospel on display for the world to see.

In this passage Paul uses an illustration that we understand. When a man and woman are married they are bound before God and the law to each other. They are not free to marry another because they have been joined together. But if one of them dies, they are released from that obligation and can marry another. Paul uses this everyday example to illustrate the truth that we have died to the law (and to sin as we learned in chapter 6) and we have been united to another husband. In a "till death do us part" moment we see that we have been parted from sin and the law through our death to them that is accomplished by Jesus. We have been united to Christ through His death and resurrection. We no longer belong to sin and we are no longer trying to earn salvation by keeping the law that we could never keep. We now belong to Jesus. We are His and He is ours.

We have died to sin and death and have been made alive with Christ (Ephesians 2:4-6). And we have been united to Him for a distinct purpose. We see in this passage the reasons. The words "in order that" and "so that" catch our attention and point to the purpose of our salvation. We have been redeemed so that we can bear fruit. We have been saved to serve Him. We have been rescued to bring Him glory.

We are not saved by our works, but our salvation should compel us to works. Not as a way to earn love from God, but as a result of the love He has given us. John Stott in response to the question of

why we serve God says, "Not because obedience leads to salvation, but because salvation leads to obedience." We have been united to Christ so that we can abide in Him and bear fruit through Him. It is not about us striving to be good in our own strength, but about being transformed into the image of the Holy One that we are united to. In marriage, husband and wife are united as one flesh. He is hers and she is his. So too in salvation as we are made one with our Savior. We are one with Him. We are His and He is ours.

When we were united with sin and living in our flesh and following our sinful desires, we were controlled by our sin. But now we have been united to Christ so that we can be controlled by the Spirit. We see here a distinction between following the law in an effort to somehow appease God and earn salvation, this is impossible legalism. In contrast we now serve God and follow His Word through the power of His Spirit. The Spirit enables in us what we could never do on our own.

Our *union with Christ* frees us from bondage to sin and to the law and frees us to service and surrender that is enabled by the Spirit of God in us.

1. How should the knowledge that we have died to sin *(Romans 6)* and died to the law *(Romans 7)* change the way that we live? How does this deepen our understanding of our new life in Christ and how we should live in light of our redemption?

2. From this passage, what is the *purpose* of our redemption?

3. How does our *union* with Christ enable us to bear fruit?

Therefore, did what is good become death to me? *Absolutely not!*
On the contrary, sin, in order to be recognized as sin, was producing
death in me through what is good, so that *through the commandment,*
sin might become sinful *beyond measure.*

ROMANS 7:13

WEEK 7 - DAY 2

THE LAW AND SIN

Read Romans 7:7-13

We have been freed from the law and made free to serve and grow in godliness. In this passage Paul brings us back to another version of the argument that he is refuting when he asks if the law is sin. He is again addressing the antinomian position that claims that the law is bad and must be totally done away with. This position is claiming that the law is the problem instead of understanding that it is sin and our own depraved hearts apart from Christ that are the problem.

In this section of Romans 7, Paul points out the function of the law. What does it do? And does this claim that it is sinful have any merit worth us considering. Paul under the inspiration of the Holy Spirit is emphatic that the answer is no.

We first see that the law exposes sin. We see clearly in Romans 7:7 that we know what sin is because of the law. As sinful people, the law of God is the standard of His perfect righteousness. It is the measurement that shows that we do not measure up. In many ways the law describes the things that we already do because of our sin nature. Paul uses the example of covetousness and tells us that it is the law that instructs us to not covet. The law of God helps us to understand and pinpoint the things in our lives that go against God's perfect and righteous law. The law exposes and reveals our sin, and ultimately that points us to our desperate need for the gospel. We are powerless and sinful, and we need a Savior to redeem us from this fallen and hopeless condition.

As the passage goes on, we see in verse 8 that the law not only exposes or reveals our sin, it also arouses sin in us. But as we look closer we can see that this arousal is in no way the fault of the law, but instead the response of our sinful hearts to the law of God. Paul uses this illustration of coveting again and says that the law produces covetousness in us. We can think of so many examples as to how this happens, though we may not like to admit that this is true of us as well. So often knowing that something is wrong or forbidden makes us want it or at the least produces a curiosity toward sin. This can be seen in young children that are told "do not touch," and they become all the more compelled to touch the forbidden object. So often we want the thing that we have been told we cannot have. We want to enter where we are told not to enter. We want to peek past the authorized personnel signs. We want to push our limits. But before we think that the law is the problem, we must be reminded that the true problem is not the law that tells us what not to do, it is our sinful and rebellious hearts that push back against the law of God. The problem is in us, not in the law.

In verses 9-11 the truth is made clear that the law condemns sin. As the law of God exposes our sin and our sinful desires allow the law to arouse sin in us, we are condemned by the law. This perfect standard of God's righteousness is one that we cannot live up to. This is in so many ways the main emphasis of the book of Romans to this point. But there is hope for broken sinners. Jesus has done what the law could never do. He has made a way for us. In His sinless life He perfectly kept the law like we never could, and in His sacrificial death He paid the price for our sins so that we could be clothed in His perfect righteousness through the gift of His grace.

Paul pulls it all together in verses 12-13 by answering his question from verse 7. Is the law sin? No, it is holy, and righteous, and good. The perfect law of God is a reflection of the Perfect One and we stand in awe before Him. The sin in us apart from Christ that is exposed, and stirs in our hearts, and ultimately is condemned in the sight of the law is not the fault of the law but is our own fault. But praise God that the gospel makes a way to be set free from the law. We are set free from the law by Jesus who has fulfilled every part of the law we could not keep.

The law exposes and reveals our sin, and ultimately that points us to our *desperate need* for the gospel.

1. In what ways does the law *reveal* or expose our sin?

2. In what ways does the law *arouse* or stir up sin in us?

3. In what way does the law *condemn* our sin?

4. How is the gospel the *answer* to the tension of sin and the law?

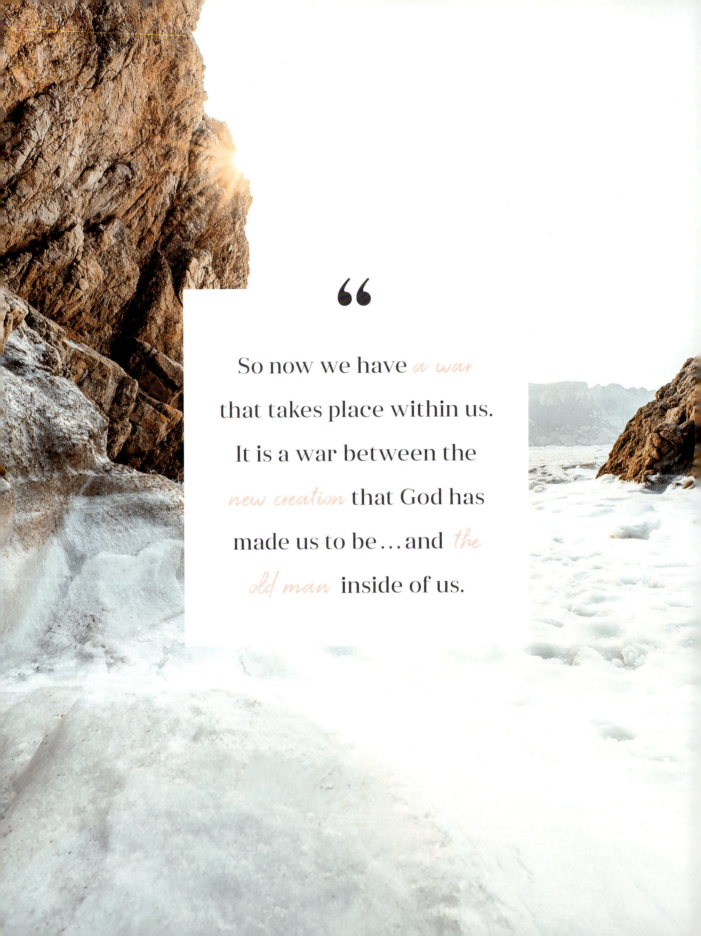

> So now we have *a war* that takes place within us. It is a war between the *new creation* that God has made us to be... and *the old man* inside of us.

WEEK 7 - DAY 3

THE STRUGGLE

Read Romans 7:14-25

The grace of God sets us free from sin and from the law. The gospel brings freedom that nothing else can bring. And yet there is an aspect of the Christian life that is a constant struggle. It is the battle between our flesh and the Spirit that is now at work within us. This is the constant battle of the Christian life. It is the now and not yet of the kingdom of God that has been inaugurated, but not yet consummated. The price for sin has been paid and death has been defeated at the cross. It is finished, and yet we wait for the completion of all things. We wait for restoration and consummation that will one day come.

Paul's words are raw and real. There is some debate among theologians as to whether these verses describe a person before salvation or after salvation. For several reasons I take the position that these verses do describe Paul after salvation as he faces that battle that wages within him. One of the biggest reasons is that before salvation, there is no battle waging within us. At the deepest level we have no desire to pursue holiness and keep the law of God before salvation. This is totally and completely the work of the Spirit working in us. In this passage Paul describes an inward battle that is not present in the heart of an unbeliever. And though we should be growing in godliness, believers will struggle with sin.

The dialogue of the passage is representative of the dialogue that so often happens in our own hearts and even in the life of the apostle Paul. As believers, we long to do what pleases God, and yet we find ourselves slipping into the same habits and sins. Paul describes it as doing the thing that we hate. Have you ever been there? Have you ever found yourself struggling with something you so desperately want to move past? Or asking, "Why did I do that?" Paul points out that it is no longer himself, but sin that is acting. He is reminding us that we have been made a new creation through Christ. We are a new person. Sin is no longer who we are, and yet still we struggle.

When we are redeemed by God's grace and born again we are made new. Before salvation, our desires were simply to please self, and even the seemingly good things that we did were done from a self-serving motive. But now as the people of God, our hearts desire is to serve God and follow His law. And though we continue to grow in grace and godliness, we will not be sinless until we are glorified in eternity. So now we have a war that takes place within us. It is a war between the new creation that God has made us to be and is continuing to form us into, and the old man inside of us.

We see Paul's frustration over his condition in verse 24, but it is quickly followed by an outburst of praise to God for the work of Jesus. Sin will be a struggle all of our lives until we see His face. But there is hope in the grace of the gospel and the finished work of the cross that has paid the price. There is hope that will not put to shame (Romans 5:5). The gospel is our hope. We don't need to work to earn God's favor or live in our own feeble strength. We can rest in His grace and the overwhelming truth of the gospel. The work of sanctification is His work. He invites us simply to surrender to His work and to see our need for His daily grace. It is then that we will be transformed by the power of His Word.

So today, we can open our Bibles. We can behold Him through His Word until the day we behold Him with our eyes. We can call to Him in adoration and confession. We can live lives not of perfection, but of repentance. We will grow in His grace little by little, moment by moment, one stumbling, limping, falling forward step at a time.

> For I know that *nothing good lives in me*, that is, in my flesh. For the desire to do what is good is with me, but there is no ability to do it.
>
> ROMANS 7:18

1. Record in the two columns below the *contrast and struggle* that take place in these verses.

OLD HEART	NEW HEART

2. How do you see this *internal struggle* play out in your own life?

3. Confession and repentance are key as we grow in godliness. What *attitude*, *action*, or *other sin* do you need to confess and repent of?

4. Spoiler alert! In context of today's reading take a peek at the next few verses in *Romans 8:1-4* and record how these verses comfort us as we battle against sin.

Therefore, there is *now no condemnation* for those in Christ Jesus

ROMANS 8:1

WEEK 7 - DAY 4

NOT GUILTY

Read Romans 8:1-2

The verdict is in. The sentence has been passed. The verdict is guilty, and the sentence is death. But as the gavel is about to come crashing down and all of our hope with it, a voice speaks grace through the chaos. There is another way. The gospel is that way. We are guilty, but the gospel is our hope. The word "gospel" means good news, and could there be any news better than this for guilty sinners condemned to death? No greater news. No greater hope. The gospel is our greatest hope and our greatest joy.

Romans 8 has been titled the greatest chapter in all of the Bible. It holds that title for good reason. Though equally inspired and necessary as every other chapter of Scripture, these 39 verses stand out as one of the most beautiful proclamations of the gospel from beginning to end. The chapter is a reminder of our status before our God. It is a call to holy living. It is hope of future glory. It is a declaration of the never-ending, never-changing, initiating love of God.

Therefore. Because of everything that you have learned in these first chapters of Romans about justification by grace, this great "therefore" begins for us a new section and proclaims a truth almost too magnificent for us to comprehend. In spite of our guilty verdict and the sentence of death that has been proclaimed, we are declared not guilty by the overflowing grace of our Savior. We are not guilty, and we are not condemned. Our sin has been washed clean and we have been clothed with the spotless righteousness of the perfect Son of God.

In previous chapters, we learned of the condemnation that comes from our position in Adam. In Adam we are made sinners, but in Christ we are justified (Romans 5:16,18). Our only hope is the cross. Our only hope is in Christ. It is through our union with Christ that we assume this status of no condemnation. Condemnation is washed away when we are united to Christ. We are not condemned. We are justified.

Not only are we no longer condemned, but the Spirit of God is at work within us. One of the key themes of this beautiful chapter is the working of the Spirit in the life of the Christian. We have been set free by the Spirit that is inside of us. The law condemns us, but the gospel sets us free. The law is the impossible standard that we cannot meet, and yet God declares over us that we are no longer condemned. Now we are free to live in the victory and forgiveness that He has shown us. If God has forgiven us and set us free, we must not stay chained to our past, but instead walk forward into the Spirit-filled life that God has called us to as new people who have been set free to serve our God.

The gospel truly is our greatest hope and our greatest joy. We should stand in awe of the life-transforming message of the gospel. We must be reminded of the depths of our sin and depravity (Romans 3:23). We must be reminded of the hopelessness of our condition (Romans 6:23). We must be reminded of the powerlessness of the law (Galatians 2:16). We must be reminded of the hope of the gospel (Romans 1:16-17). We come to chapter 8 with all of these truths imprinted on our hearts and we bow in adoration at the weight of our sin and the burden that is carried away because of Jesus. Because of Jesus, there is no condemnation for us. He was condemned so that we would not be. He has borne our griefs. He has carried our sorrows. Our iniquity has been placed on the Spotless Lamb (Isaiah 53:4-6). We stand in awe of all He has done for us. We stand in awe of the beauty of the gospel. We stand in awe of our God.

because the law of the Spirit of life in Christ Jesus has *set you free* from the law of sin and death.

ROMANS 8:2

1. *Chapter 8* begins with a "therefore." Paul is referring to everything that he has written in the book of Romans up until this point. Write a short summary of the message of Romans up until this point below.

2. Look up the word "condemnation" (or condemn) and record the meaning below. What does this tell you about our *status* before God apart from Christ?

3. What is the *significance* of the fact that it is those who are "in Christ" that are not condemned? What does this mean?

4. How should the fact that we are *no longer condemned* and that we have been set free change the way that we live?

> What the law *could not do* since it was weakened by the flesh, *God did*.
>
> ROMANS 8:3A

WEEK 7 - DAY 5

GOD HAS DONE IT

Read Romans 8:3-4

God has done it. We are free from condemnation, free from sin, and free from the law because of what God has done. This is the beauty of the gospel that captures our hearts and pulls our gaze upward. We were hopeless in our sin apart from Jesus. We were dead and unable to resurrect ourselves. The first words of Romans 8:3 pierce through the darkness of our sin with the truth that God has done it. He has done what the law could never do. We were dead in our sin (Ephesians 2:1-10) when God saved us. Of no power of our own, but only of His sovereign grace He resurrected us. In an instant, He spoke life into what was dead. We went from being spiritually dead to our lungs filling with breath and blood rushing through our veins. We cannot emphasize too much this truth. We were dead. And He made us alive.

God has done it. It is not of any doing of our own. We did not reach out for Him, He reached for us. We did not run to Him, He ran to us. He has done what the law could not do. He fulfilled the standard that we could not meet through Jesus. God Himself came in human flesh. He came in the likeness of sinful flesh. He was tempted just as we are tempted and yet never yielded to sin (Hebrews 4:15). With His perfect life, He lived the life that we could not live on our own. With His sacrificial and atoning death, He paid the price that we could never pay on our own. He did what we could never do. He accomplished what the law could never accomplish.

The answer to the problem of our sin is Jesus. He is the answer. He has satisfied the rigid demands of the law. God in His holiness cannot ignore justice. The wrath and justice of God left us condemned and without hope aside from the grace of God. But Jesus came. He came as a man. He came as God. He came to rescue and redeem His people. This justification and freedom from condemnation is possible because of our union with Christ. If we never are born again and united to Christ, we can never meet the righteous requirement of the law. The gospel compels us to place our faith in the saving grace of Jesus and His finished work at the cross. Justification is only made possible in Him. John Calvin famously said in the Institutes:

> *"We must understand that as long as Christ remains outside of us, and we are separated from him, all that he has suffered and done for the salvation of the human race remains useless and of no value to us. Therefore, to share with us what he has received from the Father, he had to become ours and to dwell within us."*

Christ in us. This is our hope. He is in us and we are in Him. Our union with Christ is the key that opens the door of salvation and of sanctification. Without union with Christ, we have no hope of salvation. Because we must be united to Him and clothed in His righteousness. And without union with Christ we have no hope of sanctification because we cannot do it on our own. Our sanctification must be a work of Christ in us. And this is the beauty of the gospel that Jesus came as a man to dwell among us (John 1:14). The language implies that He tabernacled or pitched His tent in the midst of us. He came to dwell among us so that He could dwell in us. He came to us so that we could come to Him.

Now we no longer need to be chained to sin. Though we struggle with our flesh, we also have the Spirit inside us that battles our sin for us and with us. We do not fight the battle of sin alone, the Spirit fights for us. The Spirit-filled life is one of constant surrender to the Spirit at work within us, and of day by day putting sin to death (Colossians 3:5). No condemnation is pronounced over us, and more than that is the pronouncement of righteousness. Because after we have been saved by God's grace, God no longer sees our sin, but instead sees the righteousness of Christ. Great is His Faithfulness.

> **The gospel compels us to place our faith *in the saving grace* of Jesus and His finished work at the cross. *Justification is only made possible in Him.***

1. Paraphrase *Romans 8:1-4*.

2. How does the truth that God has *accomplished* our salvation change the way that we understand the beauty of the gospel?

3. What does it mean that God has done *what the law could not do*?

4. *Sanctification* is the work of the Holy Spirit in growing us spiritually, but sometimes we think we need to make that growth happen on our own. How does union with Christ change our perspective of sanctification?

ROMANS 8:17-18

and if children, also heirs—heirs of God and coheirs with Christ—if indeed we suffer with him so that we may also be glorified with him. For I consider that the sufferings of this present time are not worth comparing with the glory that is going to be revealed to us.

WEEK SEVEN Reflection

READ ROMANS 7:1–8:4

Paraphrase the passage from this week.

What did you observe from this week's text about God and His character?

What does the passage teach about the condition of mankind and about yourself?

How does this passage point to the gospel?

How should you respond to this passage? What is the personal application?

What specific action steps can you take this week to apply the passage?

> God looks on His people and does not see the *filthy* rags of their *sin*, but the *perfect righteousness* of Jesus.

WEEK 8 - DAY 1

THE FLESH AND THE SPIRIT
Read Romans 8:5-8

There are two paths set forth in this passage. There is the path of the believer that lives a new life in the Spirit, and there is the path of the unbeliever that lives life their own way according to the desires of the flesh. Two clear paths are set before us in this passage. Paul does not show us any middle ground, or an easier option. Life in the flesh or life in the Spirit. These are the paths set before us in Romans 8.

In verse 4, Paul pointed out that the righteous requirement of the law is fulfilled in us. He is speaking here to believers. He is saying that for those that have been justified by faith in the message of the gospel of God's grace there is no condemnation. When God looks on the child of God, He does not see an enemy, but a son. He looks on His people and does not see the filthy rags of their sin, but the perfect righteousness of Jesus. The righteous requirement of the law can only be fulfilled in us if we are in Christ and He is in us. We have no righteousness in ourselves, but salvation makes us a new creation. It changes every part of us.

So, Paul contrasts for us two different types of people. Every person falls into one of these two categories. There are those that have been redeemed and live in the Spirit, and there are those still dead in their sins who live in the flesh. In justification, God changes everything about us. He changes our desires, our motives, and every single part of who we are. In contrast, living according to the flesh is living life in our own way. It is living according to a rebellious heart that has not been transformed by the grace of God.

The one that is unregenerate and living and seeking after the flesh has set their mind on the things of the flesh and the description here is characteristic of their life. The text tells us that they not only set their mind on the things of the flesh, but also that they are hostile to God, that they do not submit to God's law, and that they cannot please God. So, what exactly is the flesh? It is not the physical body. It is instead the human condition and desires apart from the regenerating work of Christ. Others may think that fleshly desires pertain simply to sexual sins, but the desires of the flesh are not limited to sins of a sexual nature. Instead, the flesh is the human nature apart from God. It is the old man.

These descriptors are impossible if the person is a believer. In Christ we are no longer the enemies of God, and there is no condemnation for us (Romans 5:2, Romans 8:1). God has transformed the hearts of believers. Before conversion we do not seek after God or desire to please Him, but after we have received His grace we are a new creation that seeks to love and serve after our Savior.

The desire to follow the Spirit is by no power of our own. It is not the result of anything good that comes from us. Instead it is the result of a righteousness that is outside of us and transferred to us. Life in the Spirit is made possible only by the saving work of Jesus Christ. We all begin in the flesh. This is who we are before salvation. But the people of God are not what they once were. The people of God have been made new and washed clean. They have been given new desires, motives, and new hearts. At their core the believer has a desire to honor God, submit to Him, and please Him. We live for His glory and not our own. We live to worship, not to earn salvation but as a result of the salvation that He has given. The end result of life in the flesh is death, but the end result of life in the Spirit is life and peace. Eternal life in eternity and peace with God then and now. The believer will not live a perfect and sinless life, but the lives of the people of God will be characterized by a desire to love, serve, and obey.

God has transformed the hearts of believers

1. *Contrast* life in the flesh with life in the Spirit.

2. How does *Romans 8:1-8* urge us to examine our hearts while also giving believers assurance?

3. This description of *unbelievers* living in the flesh is also the description of every Christian before Christ. How does understanding how far we were from God make salvation even more beautiful to you?

You, however, are *not in the flesh, but in the Spirit*, if indeed the Spirit of God lives in you. If anyone does not have the Spirit of Christ, he does not belong to him.

ROMANS 8:9

WEEK 8 - DAY 2

LIFE IN THE SPIRIT
Read Romans 8:9-11

There is another option. There is a different way. Yesterday we looked at life in the flesh. We examined the fruit of the life of an unbeliever that chooses to go their own way instead of surrendering to God. But today's passage stands in contrast to the life that is lived in the flesh, because Paul continues through the passage by turning his attention to life in the Spirit. And in this passage, Paul gets personal. He shifts his pronouns and speaks directly to us as believers. He is showing us that there is a different reality for those of us that are the children of God.

Paul tells us that as believers, we are not in the flesh, but we are in the Spirit, and the Spirit of God dwells in us. If we are believers, the Spirit of God dwells in us, and if the Spirit of God does not dwell in us, then we are not believers. This passage urges us to examine our hearts to know if we are the children of God, and yet it also urges us to complete confidence as we see the work of the Spirit in our lives (1 John 3:24). Paul contrasts for us the life in the flesh and the life in the Spirit. We were once dead in our sins, but through Jesus we have been made alive (Ephesians 2). Now we have been made alive to live a new life.

All three members of the Trinity are at work in our salvation. The Father in His initiating love has chosen us and predestined us to be His own, the Son has secured our salvation by His atoning death on the cross, and the Spirit has given us life and applied that salvation to us. Just as we are united with Christ, we are also united with the Spirit. The Spirit is in us, and we are in the Spirit. The life of the Christian is intricately bound to the Spirit of God. We experience the Spirit in the moment of salvation and every day of our lives. It is the Spirit that encourages us, convicts us, comforts us, and fills us. It is the Spirit that illuminates to us the Word of God. And the Spirit guides and directs us through every moment.

We await the consummation of what has already been accomplished. In this way this passage points us to the now and not yet of our salvation. Our salvation is secure. The Spirit dwells within us. And yet we also await the day when we will fully experience the glories of redemption. Ephesians 1:11-14 tells us that the Spirit is the guarantee or down payment of our inheritance. In this way, the Spirit of God that dwells within us is a glimpse of heaven and a glimpse of communion with God that will one day be full, complete, and unhindered by sin. All things will be made new including our bodies in eternity.

There is no condemnation for the people of God. This is the declaration that Romans 8 began with. There is no condemnation in life because Jesus

has paid the price for our salvation. There is no condemnation in death because the Spirit that has raised Jesus from the dead will also raise us as well. So, we live in light of eternity. We live in light of the sure hope that has been given to us, that just as Jesus was raised we will be raised. So, when our time on earth is ended and we close our eyes in death, we will open them to a reality more brilliant and glorious than we could have ever imagined or dreamed of. We can face both the joys and sorrows of this world in light of that truth. We can cling to the words of 1 Corinthians 2:9 that tells us that no eye has seen, or ear heard, or heart imagined what God has waiting for His people. Later in the same passage in 1 Corinthians 2:9-16, Paul makes it clear that spiritual things can only be understood by those that have been justified, united with Christ, and given the mind of Christ to see things in a new way.

The text begs for us to ask if we are indwelt by the Spirit of God. It asks if we are His. And if we are God's and His Spirit dwells within us, shouldn't this change everything about the way that we live? We must live with our hearts fixed on eternity and the glories of salvation that await us. We must live with eternity in view and our eyes transfixed on our God.

We were once dead in our sins, but through Jesus we have been made alive. Now *we have been made alive to live a new life.*

1 In *contrast* to life in the flesh, what should it look like to live life in the Spirit?

2 *Romans 8:11* tells us that the Spirit that is in us and that will raise us in eternity is the same Spirit that raised Jesus from the dead. Think about that for a moment. How does that give you confidence and assurance that God will do what He has promised?

3 How can we live with our eyes on *eternity*? What does that look like in day to day life?

"The *glorious gospel* should compel us to live a *gospel-centered* life.

WEEK 8 - DAY 3

THE MORTIFICATION OF SIN
Read Romans 8:12-13

So then. These are the words that propel us into the next portion of this beautiful chapter. You can almost hear the yearning and urgency of Paul's words. The words flow with pastoral care to his dear brothers and sisters. He has spent chapters proclaiming the truths of the gospel of God, and now he wants to make clear the implications of this gospel on our daily lives. The gospel has implications for every moment of our lives. The book of Romans is one of rich theology, but it is also one of practical Christian living. The glorious gospel should compel us to live a gospel-centered life.

So, because of the gospel. Because we have been justified by faith. Because Jesus has done what we could never do in our own strength. Because of who God is—this is how we should live. We are debtors to God alone. We owe nothing to our flesh and the sin that enslaved us. This is a declaration of war. This is a battle cry. The Christian life is one of constantly waging war against the sin in ourselves. Before our salvation, we were powerless to stop sinning. The depravity of our hearts was widespread and deadly. Sin always results in death and the sin that had infected us had spread to every crevice of our being. But God did what the law could not do and what we could not do. He reached down and rescued us.

Salvation compels us to a different kind of life. Though sin leads to death, the believer is commanded to put sin to death. We are to live in the Spirit and eradicate the sin of our hearts. Through justification, God has rendered us dead to sin, but practically, we still struggle against our sin nature until God takes it from us and glorifies us in eternity. The theological term is mortification. This is the idea of putting our sin to death (Colossians 3:5). We don't often talk about fighting against our sin. Often, we live as though we are defeated by the sins that we struggle with. We think that "this is just the way that we are." But this is anti-gospel. The message of the gospel is that we can be changed through the power of the Spirit who is at work within us. We don't muster up enough strength to change ourselves, but we cooperate with the Spirit as He transforms us into the image of Christ. We grow in godliness and grow in grace.

The command here is active and not passive. Putting our sin to death is not something that will just happen. We are commanded to put it to death. John Stott said, "There is a kind of life that leads to death, and there is a kind of death that leads to life." The life of sin leads to death, but life in the Spirit should be one of putting to death the sin that is in us.

So how does this happen? How is sin put to death in us? It must be the work of the Spirit in us. Paul says that it happens "by the Spirit." His words point us back to Romans 8:5-6 where we learned that life in the Spirit is one of setting our minds on the things of the Spirit. So often the battle begins in our minds. We must think true thoughts. We must focus our minds on gospel-truth. But this battle is also one of our hearts. It is a battle for our affections. We cannot flee from our sin if we still love it. And in order to rid ourselves of a love of sin, we must love something else more. We must love God more than we love sin. Likely we would all affirm this statement to be true, yet so often our lives contradict this statement. Our time, money, and affections reveal what is the most important thing to us. And if anything has pushed ahead of God for our affections, we must repent and return.

The battle against sin is a battle in our minds and our hearts. And the weapon that we have is clearly defined for us in Ephesians 6:17. We battle with the sword of the Spirit. We battle with the Word of God. It is the Word of God that reveals our sin, transforms our minds, and fixes our hearts on the glory of God. And as we behold Him through Scripture our hearts and minds are transformed into His image. You can be changed by God. You do not have to stay the way that you have always been. The power of the Spirit and Scripture can eradicate the sin that you struggle with.

"There is a kind of *life that leads to death*, and there is a kind of *death that leads to life.*"

— John Stott —

1. What *sin* in your life needs to be put to death?

2. In what ways can you *put to death* the sin that you wrote above?

3. The battle of sin is often the battle for our minds and for our affections. How can we love God *more than* we love our sin?

For all those led by God's Spirit are God's sons. For you did not receive a spirit of slavery to fall back into fear. Instead, you received the *Spirit of adoption*, by whom we cry out, *"Abba, Father!"*

ROMANS 8:14-15

WEEK 8 - DAY 4

ADOPTED

Read Romans 8:14-15

Romans 8 builds like a crescendo—each verse escalating with truth that brings comfort and steadfast hope to our souls. On the heels of the command to put sin to death, we come to verse 14 and a reminder that all that are led by God's Spirit are His children. Every person led by God's Spirit is a child of God and every child of God is led by the Spirit. In context of verse 13 and all that has come before these verses, it is clear that the Spirit is leading us to holiness and sanctification. So often we are tempted to wonder what God's will is for our lives, but the will of God for every child of God is holiness. We are called to be holy. We are justified to be sanctified. We are united to Christ to become like Christ.

Paul's words are emphatic to the children of God. We have not been justified to live like slaves, but like sons. The life of a slave or hired worker is one of instability. It is one of working to prove one's worth. The spirit of slavery is the attitude that we must try to earn God's love and favor. It is the disposition that leads people to try to work for their salvation. But we can never earn salvation. It can only be acquired as an unmerited gift from our gracious God. The slavery of sin has been broken and we are now the sons and daughters of God.

We do not have a spirit of slavery, but instead we have the Spirit of adoption. We have been adopted by God and made children of our Heavenly Father. The doctrine of adoption is a truth that we can rest secure in. Our adoption declares our election. We are the chosen, children of God.

In the context of the Roman culture to which Paul wrote this letter, adoption was an important part of society. Though in our western culture we primarily think of adopting babies or young children, Roman adoption was traditionally the adoption of an adult male. In some cases, this was due to the fact that a family did not have a son to further the lineage, or they did not deem their son worthy of the honor of being the future head of the family. In some ways, the honor of an adopted son was far greater than a biological son. An adopted son was one that had been chosen by the father and he would receive the full rights of a son. We did not choose to be adopted, but instead, God chooses us to be His children. We received our adoption at the time of our conversion. Through adoption we are chosen to be the Father's children. Now we live in light of that adoption. We have become sons and daughters, and we have no reason to live like slaves.

And because we have been adopted into the family of God, we now cry "Abba, Father." Abba is the term for Daddy. It shows the depth of familial love that comes with being adopted into God's family.

We are His children and we are loved with the boundless love of the perfect Father. As chosen children we call His name at every moment. In both joy and sorrow, His name is ever on our lips. In the time of the old covenant, calling God our Father was something unheard of. The Jewish people would have never presumed to call the almighty Yahweh their Father. But this is the overwhelming joy of the new covenant. In Christ we are brought near to God and we can call Him our Father. In prayer we call Him "Our Father," just as Jesus taught us to do (Matthew 6:9). Through the incarnation, the Son comes near to us and brings us close to the Father.

Our adoption changes everything. The entire Trinity is at work in our adoption. The Son pays the price for our redemption so that we can come freely to our Father and it is in the Spirit that we are adopted. Three in one and one in three, our triune God brings us near. Our assurance is rooted in our adoption and our adoption is rooted in our election. What a comfort to know that before the foundations of the world, our God has chosen us to be His own (Romans 8:29-30). We are His.

Our adoption declares our election.
We are the chosen children of God.

1. So often people want to know the will of God for their lives. How does it bring comfort to you to know that first and foremost, God's will for you is *to be like Christ*?

2. How are we often *tempted* to live like a slave instead of like a son or daughter of God?

3. How does an understanding of *Roman adoption* give you an even deeper picture of what it means to be adopted by God?

4. Because of Jesus, we can *come to God and call Him "Abba"* or "Daddy." How does Jesus change everything about the way that people relate to God?

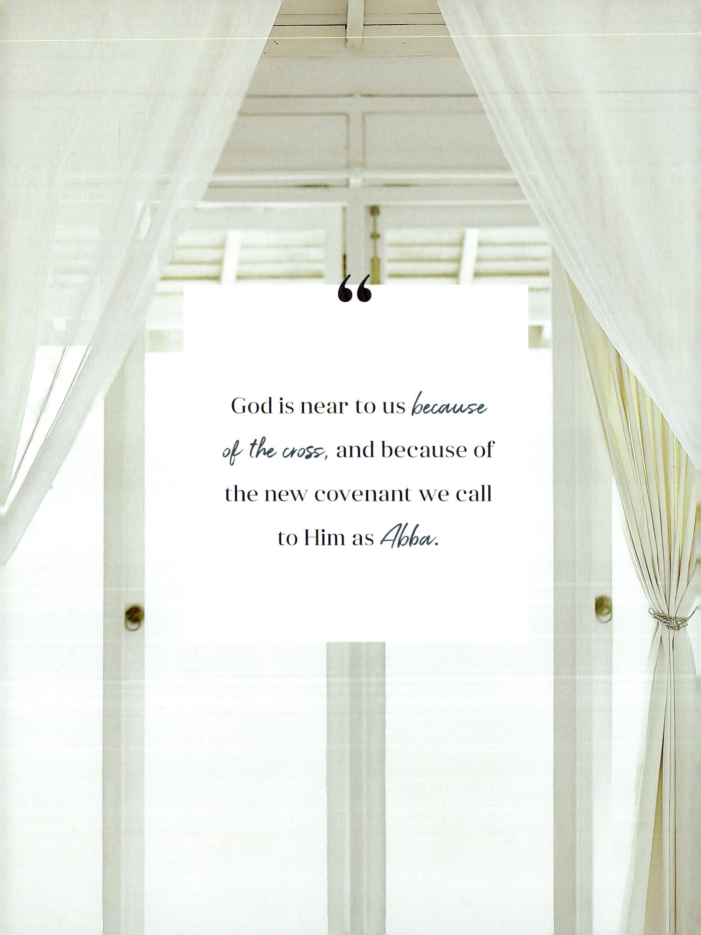

> God is near to us *because of the cross*, and because of the new covenant we call to Him as *Abba*.

WEEK 8 - DAY 5

HEIRS OF GOD

Read Romans 8:16-17

We close the first portion on our study on Romans with these gospel-saturated verses. These words bring hope to us in every season. We look on here at the results of the gospel of God that has been proclaimed in every verse of the book of Romans. We see here the confidence of our position in Christ and the privileges of salvation.

Verse 16 tells us that the Holy Spirit declares to us that we are the children of God. Many theologians connect this verse closely with verse 15 and our ability to cry "Abba" to our Father in heaven. For the children of God that have been ransomed by the blood of Christ, this confirms in us that we are God's own. God is near to us because of the cross, and because of the new covenant we call to Him as "Abba." The relationship between us and God is one of familial relationship that cannot occur apart from salvation. We see the glory of our God through His Word, we commune with Him in prayer, we are comforted by His Spirit. As the Spirit works in us, it births assurance and utter confidence that we are His.

If we have been justified by His grace, we are the children of God. And if we are the children of God than there are great privileges that come with our position in Christ. Not only are we the children of God, but we are also the heirs of God. In one sense we await the day when we receive this full inheritance. The inheritance of God Himself and unhindered fellowship in His presence. But this inheritance is not something for the future only. In a very real way, we take part in this inheritance on this earth as we experience the presence of God in our daily lives. In Ephesians 1:13-14, Paul encouraged the believers in the knowledge that they await a great inheritance, but that the Spirit of God is the guarantee or down payment of that inheritance. The Christian life lived in union with Christ and through the Spirit is a sweet glimpse of heaven. The Spirit is in us and He gives us a glimpse of what our full inheritance will one day be.

We are heirs of God. God Himself is what our hearts desire. And the joy of heaven is first and foremost that we will be in the presence of God for all eternity. We are heirs with Christ. In our union with Christ we experience all the gifts of God's grace. We are united to Christ by the power of the gospel. Ephesians 1:3 tells us that we have been blessed in Christ with every spiritual blessing. There is no blessing given to Christ that is not given to us through Him. In Him and through Him we are heirs of God.

The next privilege of salvation is likely not one that we would immediately think of as a privilege.

As children of God united to Christ, we will face suffering. The gospel is not that when we come to Christ we never face suffering, but God does transform our suffering and fill it with purpose. In John 16:33, Jesus spoke to His disciples and told them that in this world they would face suffering, but He also encouraged them to "take heart" because He had overcome the world. We will face suffering as we walk this earth. But that suffering is molding us and shaping us. It is refining our character and making us who He is creating us to be. It is making us like Him. On this earth, Jesus faced suffering that cannot be described, and we are called to share in that suffering, but we share in His suffering with hope. We have hope because we know that God is working. We have hope because the suffering that we face on this earth is nothing compared to the glory that is prepared for us (2 Corinthians 4:16-18).

And every suffering allows us to behold Him more and more and as we behold Him we are being transformed into His image (2 Corinthians 3:18). We share in His suffering because we know that we will also share in His glory.

We face every suffering of this life in hope because we know that the suffering is transforming us into the image of Christ. And though we share in His suffering here on this earth, there will come a day when we also share in the glory of the Glorious One. There will come a day when we will rejoice. We will rejoice and be glad because every moment of suffering was worth it. Every moment of sharing in His suffering will bring us to the day when we behold His glory (1 Peter 4:13). One glimpse of His glory will overwhelm us with the truth that every moment was worth it. The gospel that saves us will also bring us home.

There will come a day when we will rejoice.

1 The children of God are the heirs of God in Christ. Read *Ephesians 1:13-14*. In what ways is the Holy Spirit the down payment of our inheritance?

2 We will someday share in Christ's glory, but on this earth, we will also share in His suffering. How does an understanding that our suffering is *temporary and molding us* into the image of Christ encourage us as we walk through suffering? Refer to *James 1:2-4* and *Romans 5:1-5*.

3 What is the gospel? How has your understanding of the gospel *grown* since the beginning of the study when we asked this question on Week 1 – Day 3?

ROMANS 8:19-21

For the creation eagerly waits with anticipation for God's sons to be revealed. For the creation was subjected to futility—not willingly, but because of him who subjected it—in the hope that the creation itself will also be set free from the bondage to decay into the glorious freedom of God's children.

WEEK EIGHT *Reflection*

READ ROMANS 8:5-17

Paraphrase the passage from this week.

What did you observe from this week's text about God and His character?

What does the passage teach about the condition of mankind and about yourself?

How does this passage point to the gospel?

How should you respond to this passage? What is the personal application?

What specific action steps can you take this week to apply the passage?

OUTLINE & FLOW
of Themes in Romans

1:1-15
Paul's introduction and longing to go to Rome

1:16-17
Theme: The Gospel

1:18-3:20
The Depravity of Man: Our Condition

3:21-4:25
The Righteousness of God: Our Hope for Justification

5:1-8:39
The Triumph of Grace

9:1-11:36
The Righteousness of God to Jew and Gentile

12:1-15:13
The Grace of God in the Christian Life

15:14-16:27
God's Grace as the Gospel Goes Forth

THE ROMAN EMPIRE

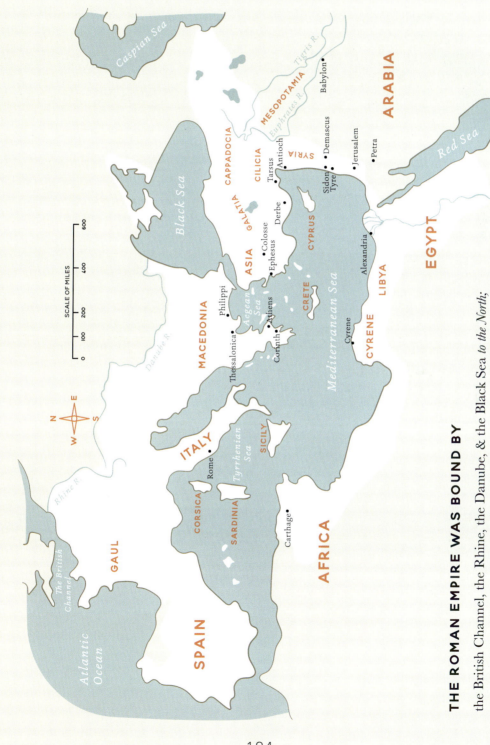

THE ROMAN EMPIRE WAS BOUND BY the British Channel, the Rhine, the Danube, & the Black Sea *to the North;* the deserts of Africa, the cataracts of the Nile, & the Arabian deserts *to the South;* the Euphrates *on the East;* the Atlantic *on the West.*

WORD STUDY

on Justification & Sin

And the gift is not like the one man's sin, because from one sin came the judgment, resulting in condemnation, but from many trespasses came the gift, resulting in justification.

ROMANS 5:16

Romans 5:16 gives us an in-depth, comprehensive look at the Gospel. In it, Paul speaks to the effect of Adam versus the effect of Christ. This verse espouses the endemic sin that is within all of humanity as effected from the Fall. It speaks to our condemnation, the curse placed on mankind because of the sin of Adam. We're also enabled to see the gift that Jesus Christ offers to us through His sacrifice on our behalf. Paul draws attention to the intrinsic state of sinfulness imparted on all people, the trespasses that we partake in, and the result of our salvation: justification.

Let's look at these concepts a little closer

SIN

Paul speaks about sin frequently throughout his letter to the Romans. In chapter 6 Paul references the ultimate sacrifice of Christ on the cross saying, "For we know that our old self was crucified with him so that the body ruled by sin might be rendered powerless so that we may no longer be enslaved to sin." Enslaved. We quickly get a picture that our sinfulness is not only bad for us, but that it owns us in some capacity. We see Paul expand on this idea in chapter 7 when he goes so far as to say that he is "of the flesh, sold as a slave to sin." Continuing on he notes that his sin nature causes him to practice what he hates and keeps him from practicing what he ought to. His sin is so endemic that it perpetually effects his behavior. In verse 17 Paul reflects that sin lives in him. *Sin is in our nature as fallen beings with Adam as our forefather.* This condition of sin within us causes us not to love God as we ought to, instead is muddles all of our affections and behavior.

TRESPASS

Let's look back at our original verse. In it, we find two specific words that we often conflate: *sin* and *trespass*. Paul used two distinct words, so we know that these definitions have a nuance to them. So, how is trespass different from sin? The denotation of this word is that regardless of intent, a mistake has been made. *More than error, a trespass is an offense.* In this case, an offense against God Himself. Paul uses this word again in 5:18 noting, "one trespass led to condemnation for all men." Through this verse we see the weightiness of trespassing against God—betraying and offending God condemns us. But Paul doesn't end his remarks of the gravity of our sinful nature and trespasses here.

JUSTIFICATION

Justification is tied directly to righteousness and has a legal connotation to it. Paul uses this word throughout Romans as a declaration of righteousness (Romans 1:32 uses 'just sentence,' 2:26 uses 'law's requirements'). Justification is a statement of innocence by a judge. Throughout this letter, Paul uses the term "justification" to convey our position after salvation; we are declared innocent through the blood of Jesus Christ. *Distinct from sanctification (growth toward holiness) justification is effective immediately in salvation.*

In 5:16, Paul speaks about sin, trespass, and justification in light of one thing: a gift. This is the gift of salvation offered to us from Jesus Christ because of His sacrifice on the cross. Despite our sinful state inherited from Adam and despite our many and continual offenses toward Him, God as our perfect, just judge has declared us innocent. Though our lives and actions might declare otherwise, God has imparted righteousness on us.

Echoes of Israel in the Roman Church

In Romans 2:12-29 Paul begins to speak about "the law." Now, he is not referencing the Roman's legal or court systems, instead he is referencing Jewish heritage. Broadly, the law is the Old Testament, more specifically it is considered the first five books of the Bible: Genesis, Exodus, Leviticus, Numbers, and Deuteronomy. These books not only tell the story of the formation of Israel as God's people, but it also gives an in-depth legal code by which the Israelites were expected to abide. These laws were meant to set Israel apart from the surrounding nations, calling them to high standards of ethical integrity. These ordinances had a major function of making Israel pure; God could not dwell with His people if sins were left unconfessed and unatoned or if there were symbols of death and sin all around.

ROMANS 2:12-13

All who sin without the law will also perish without the law, and all who sin under the law will be judged by the law. For the hearers of the law are not righteous before God, but the doers of the law will be justified.

BROADLY
the law is the Old Testament

MORE SPECIFICALLY
it is considered the first five books of the Bible: Genesis, Exodus, Leviticus, Numbers, and Deuteronomy.

We often see that the law was a good thing (for example, 1 Timothy 1:8, Psalm 119:30). It made Israel distinct, allowing for a way for a holy and pure God to dwell in the presence of His people, and it proclaimed a message to onlookers that purity is important. But in Romans, Paul seems to be making a distinction about the purpose of the law. Not only does Paul make a point to say that the law itself does not impart righteousness on those who obey it, but he furthers his point by saying the Gentiles (who weren't a part of Israel and thereby did not have access to the law) have the law written on their hearts, which condemns them as guilty.

ROMANS 2:28-29

For a person is not a Jew who is one outwardly, and true circumcision is not something visible in the flesh. On the contrary, a person is a Jew who is one inwardly, and circumcision is of the heart—by the Spirit, not the letter. That person's praise is not from people but from God.

Toward the end of this passage, Paul brings up a specific ordinance of the law: circumcision. Circumcision was a gesture that began in Genesis 17 when God made a covenant with Abraham. A physical sign of the covenant was the act of circumcision on all males belonging to God's chosen people, Abraham's family. From the book of Galatians, we know that circumcision was still a controversial subject in the early church. Through His sacrifice, Jesus had offered salvation to all, including the Gentiles. Yet, there were many Jews still preaching circumcision. Despite the new and better covenant that had been made though Jesus, there were still many who preached that circumcision was necessary for salvation.

FIRST MENTION OF CIRCUMCISION - Genesis 17:10-14

Paul responded to this folly in Romans 2:25-29. True circumcision, that is true covenant relationship with God, is not visible, physical, or outward. Our circumcision in Christ is a circumcision of our hearts by the power of the Holy Spirit within us. Paul's statement declares that salvation is open to all, Jews and Gentiles alike.

Neither circumcision nor the law saves us, it is only through a covenantal relationship with Jesus Christ.

Through his letter to the Romans, Paul is trying to shift the paradigm of what the purpose of the law is in light of Jesus. The law is still important; we still need to read the Old Testament. But, we do so having read about the immense sacrifice of Jesus. The covenant that we have with Jesus is superior to any covenant we could have spilled our own blood on from circumcision. Jesus provided a better way, a new covenant in which we are freed from the bondage of sin by His comprehensive, perfect, unrelenting sacrifice.

ADAM AND CHRIST

Romans 5:12-21

ADAM	JESUS
Sin and death entered into the world through Adam	Abundance of grace and the free gift of righteousness through Jesus
One trespass led to condemnation through Adam	Jesus' one act of righteousness leads to justification and life for all men
By Adam's rebellion, many were made sinners	By Jesus' obedience many will be made righteous

so that, just as sin reigned in death, so also grace will reign through righteousness, resulting in eternal life through Jesus Christ our Lord.

ROMANS 5:21

GLOSSARY *of* TERMS

FAITH

The concept of hopeful trust in the Lord because of a proper knowledge of His character.

Hebrews 11:1

GOSPEL

The good news of salvation, that Jesus Christ died, was buried, and resurrected from the grave defeating sin and death on our behalf and offering us eternal life and a personal relationship with Him.

Ephesians 1:13

GRACE

God's forgiving mercy; not receiving what our sins deserve.

Ephesians 2:5

JUSTIFY/ JUSTIFICATION

Being declared as innocent by a Judge.

Galatians 2:16

PROPITIATION/ ATONEMENT

A pardoning from sin through a sacrifice.

1 John 2:2

RECONCILED/ RECONCILIATION

To resolve a relationship that was once at odds.

Col 1:21-22

REPENTANCE

Realizing sinfulness, fleeing sinfulness, and pursuing holiness.

Psalm 51:4

SALVATION

Liberation from sin or guilt.

Exodus 14:13

SANCTIFICATION

The Holy Spirit working within a Christian toward continual spiritual growth.

2 Thessalonians 2:13

FOR STUDYING GOD'S
WORD WITH US!

CONNECT WITH US:

@THEDAILYGRACECO

@KRISTINSCHMUCKER

CONTACT US:

INFO@THEDAILYGRACECO.COM

SHARE:

#THEDAILYGRACECO

#LAMPANDLIGHT

WEBSITE:

WWW.THEDAILYGRACECO.COM